JAMESTOWN  PUBLISHERS

Themes *in* Reading

VOLUME *1*

A MULTICULTURAL COLLECTION

DISCARD

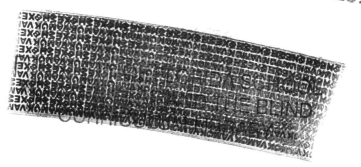

Editorial Director: Cynthia Krejcsi

Executive Editor: Marilyn Cunningham

Design Manager: Ophelia M. Chambliss

Production and Design: PiperStudiosInc .

Cover and Interior Illustration: Jason O'Malley

Production Manager: Margo Goia

ISBN: 0-89061-811-9

Published by Jamestown Publishers,

a division of NTC/Contemporary Publishing Company,

4255 West Touhy Avenue,

Lincolnwood (Chicago), Illinois 60646-1975, U.S.A.

JAMESTOWN  PUBLISHERS

Themes *in* Reading

VOLUME 1

A MULTICULTURAL COLLECTION

JAMESTOWN PUBLISHERS

A DIVISION OF NTC/CONTEMPORARY
PUBLISHING COMPANY

Contents

Unit 1: Accomplishments

Unit 2: Acts of Kindness

Unit 3: Communication

Unit 4: Decisions

Accomplishments

Accomplishments can be great or small. Winning a gold medal in the Olympics is an accomplishment. So is learning to play the piano well or making the baseball team or even getting your homework done on time.

Accomplishing something usually takes determination and hard work but makes people feel good about themselves. Think about an accomplishment you are proud of. What makes it so special?

In this unit you will read about people who succeeded in accomplishing their dreams or goals. In doing so, they gained a great deal of personal satisfaction and in some cases inspired others to work hard to reach their own goals.

As you read, think about your goals and dreams—those you had in the past and those you have now. Think about why they are important to you.

Yes, It Was My Grandmother

Luci Tapahonso

Are you like one of your relatives? See why this Native American poet thinks she is like her grandmother.

Yes, it was my grandmother
who trained wild horses for pleasure and pay.
People knew of her, saying:

> She knows how to handle them.
> Horses obey that woman.

She worked,
skirts flying, hair tied securely in the wind and dust.
She rode those animals hard and was thrown,
time and time again.
She worked until they were meek
and wanting to please.

> She came home at dusk,
> tired and dusty,
> smelling of sweat and horses.

She couldn't cook,
my father said smiling,
your grandmother hated to cook.

Oh Grandmother,
who freed me from cooking.
Grandmother, you must have made sure
I met a man who would not share the
kitchen.

I am small like you and
do not protect my careless hair
from wind or rain—it tangles often,
Grandma, and it is wild and untrained.

About the Author

Luci Tapahonso, a member of the Navajo Nation, was born in Shiprock, New Mexico, in 1953. She is an associate professor of English at the University of Kansas and the author of four collections of poetry, including *A Breeze Swept Through* (1987), and numerous children's books. She has also been the poet in residence at the Robert Frost Place, which annually honors a distinguished poet.

Responding to the Poem

▼ Think Back

What kind of woman is the speaker's grandmother?

How does the speaker feel about her grandmother? What details give you clues about her feelings?

In what ways is the speaker like her grandmother?

▼ Discuss

Which of your relatives are you most like? Which relative has influenced your life? Explain how you are alike or how that person influenced you.

How did the speaker learn about her grandmother? What else might she want to say to her grandmother? Why do you think Luci Tapahonso wrote this poem?

▼ Write

Describe a Person Luci Tapahonso uses descriptive language to give readers a mental picture of the speaker's grandmother and to help them better understand and know her. Use descriptive language to write a paragraph or two about someone you know and admire.

Write a Poem Using "Yes, It Was My Grandmother" as a model, expand your description into a poem. Develop your poem by combining details from the description with your feelings about the person.

The Scholarship Jacket

Marta Salinas

When you win a prize, should you have to pay for it? Decide whether you agree with the principal or with Martha's grandfather.

The small Texas school that I attended carried out a tradition every year during the eighth grade graduation; a beautiful gold and green jacket, the school colors, was awarded to the class valedictorian, the student who had maintained the highest grades for eight years. The scholarship jacket had a big gold S on the left front side and the winner's name was written in gold letters on the pocket.

My oldest sister Rosie had won the jacket a few years back and I fully expected to win also. I was fourteen and in the eighth grade. I had been a straight A student since the first grade, and the last year I had looked forward to owning that jacket. My father was a farm laborer who couldn't earn enough money to feed eight children, so when I was six I was given to my grandparents to raise. We couldn't participate in sports at school because there were registration fees, uniform costs, and trips out of town; so even though we were quite agile and athletic, there would never be a sports school jacket for us. This one, the scholarship jacket, was our only chance.

In May, close to graduation, spring fever struck, and no one paid any attention in class; instead we stared out the windows and at each other, wanting to speed up the last few weeks of school. I despaired[1] every time I looked in the mirror. Pencil thin, not a curve anywhere, I was called "Beanpole" and "String Bean" and I knew that's what I looked like. A flat chest, no hips, and a brain, that's what I had. That really isn't much for a fourteen-year-old to work with, I thought, as I absentmindedly wandered from my history class to the gym. Another hour of sweating in basketball and displaying my toothpick legs was coming up. Then I remembered my P.E. shorts were still in a bag under my desk where I'd forgotten them. I had to walk all the way back and get them. Coach Thompson was a real bear if anyone wasn't dressed for P.E. She had said I was a good forward and once she even tried to talk Grandma into letting me join the team. Grandma, of course, said no.

I was almost back at my classroom's door when I heard angry voices and arguing. I stopped. I didn't mean to eavesdrop;[2] I just hesitated, not knowing what to do. I needed those shorts and I was going to be late, but I didn't want to interrupt an argument between my teachers. I recognized the voices: Mr. Schmidt, my history teacher, and Mr. Boone, my math teacher. They seemed to be arguing about me. I couldn't believe it. I still remember the shock that rooted me flat against the

[1] felt hopeless

[2] listen secretly to what is said in private

wall as if I were trying to blend in with the graffiti written there.

"I refuse to do it! I don't care who her father is, her grades don't even begin to compare to Martha's. I won't lie or falsify records. Martha has a straight A plus average and you know it." That was Mr. Schmidt and he sounded very angry. Mr. Boone's voice sounded calm and quiet.

"Look, Joann's father is not only on the Board, he owns the only store in town; we could say it was a close tie and—"

The pounding in my ears drowned out the rest of the words, only a word here and there filtered through. ". . . Martha is Mexican. . . . resign. . . . won't do it. . . ." Mr. Schmidt came rushing out, and luckily for me went down the opposite way toward the auditorium, so he didn't see me. Shaking, I waited a few minutes and then went in and grabbed my bag and fled from the room. Mr. Boone looked up when I came in but didn't say anything. To this day I don't remember if I got in trouble in P.E. for being late or how I made it through the rest of the afternoon. I went home very sad and cried into my pillow that night so Grandmother wouldn't hear me. It seemed a cruel coincidence[3] that I had overheard that conversation.

[3] event that happens at the same time as another by accident

The next day when the principal called me into his office, I knew what it would be about. He looked uncomfortable and unhappy. I decided I wasn't going to make it any easier for him so I looked him straight in the eye. He looked away and fidgeted with the papers on his desk.

"Martha," he said, "there's been a change in policy[4] this year regarding the scholarship jacket. As you know, it has always been free." He cleared his throat and continued. "This year the Board decided to charge fifteen dollars—which still won't cover the complete cost of the jacket."

I stared at him in shock and a small sound of dismay escaped my throat. I hadn't expected this. He still avoided looking in my eyes.

"So if you are unable to pay the fifteen dollars for the jacket, it will be given to the next one in line."

Standing with all the dignity I could muster,[5] I said, "I'll speak to my grandfather about it, sir, and let you know tomorrow." I cried on the walk home from the bus stop. The dirt road was a quarter of a mile from the highway, so by the time I got home, my eyes were red and puffy.

"Where's Grandpa?" I asked Grandma, looking down at the floor so she wouldn't ask me why I'd been crying. She was sewing on a quilt and didn't look up.

"I think he's out back working in the bean field."

I went outside and looked out at the fields. There he was. I could see him walking between the rows, his body bent over the little plants, hoe in hand. I walked slowly out to him, trying to think how I could best ask him for the money. There was a cool breeze blowing and a sweet smell of mesquite[6] in the air, but I didn't appreciate it. I kicked at a dirt clod. I wanted that jacket so much. It

[4] rules or regulations that guide decisions

[5] call forth

[6] a spiny tree or shrub with sweet pods that farm animals eat

was more than just being a valedictorian and giving a little thank you speech for the jacket on graduation night. It represented eight years of hard work and expectation. I knew I had to be honest with Grandpa; it was my only chance. He saw me and looked up.

He waited for me to speak. I cleared my throat nervously and clasped my hands behind my back so he couldn't see them shaking. "Grandpa, I have a big favor to ask you," I said in Spanish, the only language he knew. He still waited silently. I tried again. "Grandpa, this year the principal said the scholarship jacket is not going to be free. It's going to cost fifteen dollars and I have to take the money in tomorrow, otherwise it'll be given to someone else." The last words came out in an eager rush. Grandpa straightened up tiredly and leaned his chin on the hoe handle. He looked out over the field that was filled with the tiny green bean plants. I waited, desperately hoping he'd say I could have the money.

He turned to me and asked quietly, "What does a scholarship jacket mean?"

I answered quickly; maybe there was a chance. "It means you've earned it by having the highest grades for eight years and that's why they're giving it to you." Too late I realized the significance[7] of my words. Grandpa knew that I understood it was not a matter of money. It wasn't that. He went back to hoeing the weeds that sprang up between the delicate little bean plants. It was a time consuming job; sometimes the small shoots were right next to each other. Finally he spoke again.

[7] importance

"Then if you pay for it, Marta, it's not a scholarship jacket, is it? Tell your principal I will not pay the fifteen dollars."

I walked back to the house and locked myself in the bathroom for a long time. I was angry with Grandfather even though I knew he was right, and I was angry with the Board, whoever they were. Why did they have to change the rules just when it was my turn to win the jacket?

[8] not wanting to communicate

It was a very sad and withdrawn[8] girl who dragged into the principal's office the next day. This time he did look me in the eyes.

"What did your grandfather say?"

I sat very straight in my chair.

"He said to tell you he won't pay the fifteen dollars."

The principal muttered something I couldn't understand under his breath, and walked over to the window. He stood looking out at something outside. He looked bigger than usual when he stood up; he was a tall gaunt[9] man with gray hair, and I watched the back of his head while I waited for him to speak.

[9] very thin

"Why?" he finally asked. "Your grandfather has the money. Doesn't he own a small bean farm?"

I looked at him, forcing my eyes to stay dry. "He said if I had to pay for it, then it wouldn't be a scholarship jacket," I said and stood up to leave. "I guess you'll just have to give it to Joann." I hadn't meant to say that; it had just slipped out. I was almost to the door when he stopped me.

"Martha—wait."

I turned and looked at him, waiting. What did he want now? I could feel my heart pounding. Something bitter and vile[10] tasting was coming up in my mouth; I was afraid I was going to be sick. I didn't need any sympathy speeches. He sighed loudly and went back to his big desk. He looked at me, biting his lip, as if thinking.

[10] disgusting

"Okay, damn it. We'll make an exception in your case. I'll tell the Board, you'll get your jacket."

I could hardly believe it. I spoke in a trembling rush. "Oh, thank you, sir!" Suddenly I felt great. I didn't know about adrenaline[11] in those days, but I knew something was pumping through me, making me feel as tall as the sky. I wanted to yell, jump, run the mile, do something. I ran out so I could cry in the hall where there was no one to see me. At the end of the day, Mr. Schmidt winked at me and said, "I hear you're getting a scholarship jacket this year."

[11] a natural substance within the body that causes it to react to stress by raising blood pressure and heart rate

His face looked as happy and innocent as a baby's, but I knew better. Without answering I gave him a quick hug and ran to the bus. I cried on the walk home again, but this time because I was so happy. I couldn't wait to tell Grandpa and ran straight to the field. I joined him in the row where he was working and without saying anything I crouched down and started pulling up the weeds with my hands. Grandpa worked alongside me for a few minutes, but he didn't ask what had happened. After I had a little pile of weeds between the rows, I stood up and faced him.

"The principal said he's making an exception for me, Grandpa, and I'm getting the jacket after all. That's after I told him what you said."

Grandpa didn't say anything, he just gave me a pat on the shoulder and a smile. He pulled out the crumpled red handkerchief that he always carried in his back pocket and wiped the sweat off his forehead.

"Better go see if your grandmother needs any help with supper."

I gave him a big grin. He didn't fool me. I skipped and ran back to the house whistling some silly tune.

About the Author

Marta Salinas was born in Mexico and now lives in the United States. She writes for newspapers and magazines such as the *Los Angeles Herald Examiner* and *California Living*. Her works have also been published in anthologies. "The Scholarship Jacket" is from *Growing Up Chicana/o*.

Responding to the Story

▼ Think Back

Why was the scholarship jacket important to Martha?

What were Mr. Boone and Mr. Schmidt arguing about? Why did Mr. Boone want to give the jacket to Joann instead of to Martha?

Why did Martha's grandfather refuse to pay fifteen dollars for the jacket?

▼ Discuss

What did Martha learn from this incident? What is the real meaning of scholarship or other achievement awards? What awards do you value?

Why did the principal change his mind and decide to give the jacket to Martha? What is your opinion of the principal? List at least three qualities a principal should possess.

▼ Write

Write a Scene Would you have kept quiet as Martha did when she heard her teachers arguing about her? Why or why not? Write a scene using dialogue that describes what you think Martha might have said.

Fill in the Blanks Who do you think convinced the principal to charge fifteen dollars for the jacket? Write a conversation that might have taken place between that person and the principal.

That Something Special: Dancing with the Repertory[1] Dance Company of Harlem

Leslie Rivera

Each of us has something we are good at. What does the poet think is special about herself?

[1] a collection of musical or theatrical works performed by a particular person or group

They tell me
that I have that something special.
But I don't see it the way they do.
That something
is what I give to them
my audience
and what I get back in return
is amazing.
I pour out my heart,
my soul, and every little dream
that I have.
People see it
and respond.
It is the sole reason I dance.

It is my way of reaching out
touching the world
letting it see my dreams and hopes.
It's that something special
that makes me give to my audiences
that makes them know what I feel.
And for them to see that
is an accomplishment all its own.

About the Author

Leslie Rivera was lucky enough to be chosen as one of twelve eighth-grade girls who took part in a special literature project in their New York neighborhood. The group met with authors and teachers who encouraged them to read and critique the works of writers with similar backgrounds and also to write and edit poetry and short stories about their own experiences. Their finished works were published in the book *Hispanic, Female and Young: An Anthology.*

Responding to the Poem

▼ Think Back

Why does the speaker dance?

What is "that something special"?

What does the speaker say is the audience's accomplishment?

▼ Discuss

The speaker refers to dancing as a way to communicate to her audience. Do you agree with her? In what ways might a dancer communicate with an audience?

If you were Rivera, which would you be prouder of, your dancing abilities or your relationship with the audience? Which is a more satisfying accomplishment? Why?

▼ Write

Freewrite How do you share a skill, a talent, or a special interest with others? Write down every thought that comes into your head about what you do. Think about how your sharing makes you and others feel.

Write a Poem "That Something Special" is written in free verse. The poem seems to flow naturally from one idea to the next. Using the thoughts and ideas from your freewriting activity, write a poem about your special talent or interest.

The Contest

Janet Stevenson

Marian Anderson was one of the greatest concert singers of the twentieth century. Before achieving worldwide fame, she took part in many voice contests. In 1925 her teacher entered her in a contest for an appearance at Lewisohn Stadium in New York City. Before the tryouts, held in New York's Aeolian Hall, Marian's teacher gave her some advice.

What part do teachers and coaches play in helping talented people accomplish their goals?

E very one of the contestants—and there were 300 of them—had an accompanist,[1] and most had a teacher with them too. The crowd filled the whole ground floor of Aeolian Hall.

At the appointed hour, the rules were announced over a public address system from the balcony, where the judges sat—heard but not seen. They explained that there was not time for each contestant to sing all the material he or she had prepared. The judges would listen to what they felt to be a fair sample. Then a clicker would sound. The singer was to stop and leave the stage.

[1] one who plays the piano or other instrument to back up a singer

"Pay no attention," Mr. Boghetti whispered in Marian's ear. "If they stop you, pretend you don't hear. Go on to the end. Be sure you get in that final trill."

"Go on singing when they tell me to stop?"

Marian was appalled² at such boldness, but Mr. Boghetti believed in boldness.

"Not for everybody, maybe. But for you. You must insist that they hear you out."

Marian said nothing, but she didn't believe she could do what he was asking. Hard as it was to disobey her teacher, it would be harder to disobey the unseen judges.

Meanwhile she had drawn a number and was waiting her turn. By the time it came near, several other singers had sung her Donizetti aria.³ Not one of them had got to the final trill. Each time the clicker cut short their song, Marian winced. Each time she winced, Mr. Boghetti glared a warning at her.

³ main song

"What if I skip the recitative⁴ and start with the aria itself?" she whispered.

⁴ speaking part

He shook his head. "Sing it all. Make them listen!"

The next contestants got only a minute or two apiece. It was her turn.

She began with the half-spoken recitative, though it seemed a waste of precious time. She could feel her teacher's hypnotic eye on her, reminding her of his command. She was expecting at any instant the sound of the clicker and the awful decision—which command to disobey?

But the clicker didn't sound.

Maybe she didn't hear it. (Her ears had felt a little dull since her last ducking in the Y pool.) She was well into the aria now! Singing as if each note might be the last—as indeed it might! On and on to the great final trill! She sang it through to the last beautiful flourish!

There was a second of dead silence. Then applause broke out all over Aeolian Hall.

———————

    She was well into the
  aria now! Singing as if
   each note might be the
  last—as indeed it might!

———————

An angry voice on the loud speaker reminded the audience that applause was forbidden. Then it asked Marian whether she had another song.

She sang one of her English songs, and went back to her seat.

"Did the clicker sound?" she asked Mr. Boghetti.

"No! You are the only who who has finished the aria! Not to speak of a second song!"

They left soon afterwards to catch the train back to Philadelphia. Mr. Boghetti was elated by her success, but as always he found things that could be improved. He talked about them all the way home, which gave Marian a chance to relax and become aware of something very peculiar about one of her ears.

It was not so much pain as a sort of numbness. She said nothing about it. She had never mentioned the swimming lessons to Mr. Boghetti and she suspected that he was not going to approve. Not if the trouble in her ear had anything to do with them.

Perhaps it would be better to give up swimming.

Two days later Mr. Boghetti called her on the phone.

"You have won!"

"Won?"

"You are one of 16 who will sing in the semifinals. Four will be chosen from them."

So it was back to work in the muggy heat. Marian was almost tempted to go back to the Y pool, just to cool off a little, but her ear still felt strange. She thought once of going to a doctor, but it got no worse, and she really had no time to spare.

On the second trip to New York, Mr. Boghetti was full of ambitious[5] hopes. He was talking about how he would coach Marian for the Lewisohn Stadium appearance, assuming that she would win today's round, and go on to win the finals. Marian wished she could share his enthusiasm, but she felt wooden beside him.

In fact she felt worse than wooden. Her ear was beginning to hurt.

She had thought when she got up this morning that there was something stuck in it. Perhaps it was one of the little cotton plugs she had used to keep the water

[5] high; expecting the best

out while she swam. She tried pulling it out, first with her fingers, then with tweezers, but working at it made it worse.

By the time they got to Aeolian Hall, she had a real old-fashioned earache. Not unbearable yet, but getting worse.

"It won't be so long today," Mr. Boghetti said cheerfully. "There are only 16 contestants. You may be one of the first."

Marian hoped so. She was not sure how long she could hold out. But Mr. Boghetti was right; she was called after only a half hour's wait.

She had to sing her aria and both her other songs. As soon as she was through, Mr. Boghetti took her back to his studio to rest until train time.

"Why do you look so discouraged?" he asked. "You did well. Very well!"

Marian was tempted to tell him that it was not discouragement he saw on her face. But it had got too bad to talk about at all. She felt as if there were some horrible growth deep inside her ear. Her hearing was affected. What if it turned out to be permanent? Beethoven had gone deaf, and he had gone on composing and conducting, but who ever heard of a deaf singer?

The phone rang and Mr. Boghetti answered it.

"What? . . . Are you sure? . . . All right, all right!"

He turned back to Marian with a dazed look, which could be the shock of joy or the shock of defeat.

"There are to be no finals," he said. "It is unanimous.[6] You will sing on August 25th at Lewisohn Stadium!"

At that moment Marian was wondering whether she would ever sing anywhere again.

But the growth in her ear was only an abscess.[7] As soon as it was lanced[8] and the pressure relieved, the pain began to ease.

"Will I be deaf?" she asked the doctor.

"Not if you take care of yourself, and stay out of swimming pools for the rest of the summer."

Orders she didn't mind obeying for the rest of that summer and several summers to come!

About the Author

Janet Stevenson has written plays, as well as novels and biographies. "The Contest" is an excerpt from *Singing to the World,* her biography of Marian Anderson. While doing research for the book, Ms. Stevenson was able to visit Marian Anderson in her Philadelphia home.

Responding to the Biography

▼ Think Back

How many people competed in the first round of the contest? How many contestants were in the semifinals?

What difficulty did Marian have to overcome on her trip to New York City for the semifinals?

What thoughts were going through Marian's mind as she waited to hear the results of the semifinals?

▼ Discuss

What part did Mr. Boghetti play in Marian's accomplishments? Do you think he gave her good advice when he told her to disobey the judges? Explain.

Which of Marian's accomplishments was greater—winning over so many other contestants or overcoming her painful ear abscess? Why do you think as you do?

▼ Write

Write a Summary The author relates some important events in Marian Anderson's life in chronological order—the order in which they occurred. Write a brief summary of "The Contest," describing the events in chronological order.

Track Your Life List some events that happened to you in the last week in chronological order. Refer to your list to write a short account of your week.

Beautiful Junk

A Story of the Watts Towers

Jon Madian

With a lot of hard work, Simon Rodia made a dream come true. What do you think of his accomplishment?

Charlie didn't notice the colors of the sun setting behind the telephone lines. The alley was cool and dark in the shadows of evening. Charlie crouched near some trash cans and raised a steel pipe high above his head.

"Junk, dirty junk!" he growled. And the pipe hit the waiting bottle, exploding glass in a hundred directions.

Pipe in hand, Charlie moved through the shadows to a trash can where he took another bottle. Crouching, he put it on the pavement. "Junk, junk, dirty junk!" he shouted, his pipe striking again and again. Then he pounded the pavement harder and yelled louder, "Junk! Junk! Dirty, dirty junk!"

Charlie was so busy pounding and shouting, he didn't notice the old man who came around the corner pushing a wheelbarrow. The wheelbarrow was full of empty bottles, rusted wire, and other junk collected from the back alleys.

The old man stopped and watched. When Charlie was tired of banging, he looked up. He was surprised and frightened. The old man was looking down at him.

"W-w-what do you want?" Charlie stammered.

"Some bottles and wire," said the old man in a quiet voice. "But I see you've broken all the bottles. Did you see any wire in the trash cans?"

"Why do you want bottles and wire?" asked Charlie. "You get money for 'em?"

"No," answered the old man.

Then he bent over and looked at the broken pieces of glass at Charlie's feet.

"May I have some of these?" he asked.

"You want that junk?" Charlie asked, sneering in disbelief. "Sure, take it."

The old man picked out pieces of blue, green, and rust colored glass. Then he took a brown bag from his pocket, unfolded it, and carefully placed the pieces of glass inside.

"Man, who ever heard of collectin' busted-up glass," said Charlie.

"Some of these pieces are beautiful. You broke them into fine shapes."

"Beautiful!" exclaimed Charlie with a laugh. "You must be blind. That glass is junk. Ugly junk, like everything in this alley, and everything in your broken-down old wheelbarrow."

The old man looked at his wheelbarrow, then he looked at Charlie.

"Maybe you're right," he said. He bent over the wheelbarrow and started down the shadowy alley.

———————

"Beautiful junk! Beautiful
junk! Crazy old man thinks
junk is beautiful!"

———————

A few days later, as Charlie left school with his friend Sammy, he saw the old man across the street. The old man's wheelbarrow was heaped full of broken dishes and rusted pipes, and tied on the top was a metal gate.

Charlie pointed. "He thinks broken junk is beautiful." Then cupping his hands to his mouth, Charlie shouted, "Beautiful junk! Beautiful junk! Crazy old man thinks junk is beautiful!"

The boys laughed and jeered. The old man walked on.

Charlie didn't see the old man again for many weeks, and he had almost forgotten about him.

Then one evening he and Sammy were playing in a vacant lot. They'd found some old, thrown away records. They tied the records to a string and shot at them with slingshots.

As they were taking aim, the old man came around the corner. The boys spoke loudly. "Now look at that beautiful record!" They opened fire. The rocks whizzed through the air and smashed the records to pieces.

"You're good shots," said the old man.

"We like to break records," said Charlie.

"I hope you won't break them all."

"Why not?" asked Sammy. "They're no good to no one. They're all scratched."

"Because . . ." began the old man.

" 'Cause he thinks they're beautiful," interrupted Charlie.

"Yes, I think so. I can use them even if they're scratched."

"What's pretty 'bout a busted-up black record?" demanded Charlie.

"Its shape. Its shape is perfect," said the old man. "Can you think of anything else that has so many perfect circles, one right next to the other?"

After a moment, Charlie said, "I bet you want a record."

"I would use it."

Charlie handed him a record, and the old man went on his way down the alley.

"He's a crazy man!" exclaimed Charlie, looking after him.

"Crazy as a witch on Halloween!" Sammy agreed.

"But where would that crazy man take all of that junk?" asked Charlie.

And the boys gathered some more stones.

The old man must be crazy, thought Charlie as he lay in bed that night. Tomorrow I'll follow him and see what he does with all that junk.

After school, Charlie and Sammy played in the vacant lot, but the old man didn't come by. All that week and the first part of the next week, Charlie searched the streets near his home.

Finally, on Wednesday, while he was eating lunch with Sammy, Charlie saw the old man pushing his empty wheelbarrow outside the school fence.

"There he is!" Charlie pointed. "Let's follow him!"

"We can't!" exclaimed Sammy. "We got to stay in school!"

"I'm not stayin'. Come on, now's our chance!" Charlie insisted.

"And get picked up by the police for cuttin', not me!" Sammy answered.

"Okay, if you're scared, I'll follow him myself," said Charlie, and he climbed the fence and started after the old man.

Charlie stayed a good distance behind so he wouldn't be seen. The old man turned into an alley and stopped by some trash cans. Carefully, he looked through the things in one of the cans. He chose a bottle, held it up to the sun, spun it around, laughed and mumbled, and placed it in his wheelbarrow.

He's a crazy man for sure, thought Charlie. I better not let him catch me.

The school bell rang in the distance. Suddenly, it was quiet in the alley. Charlie was crouching and hiding, while the old man was staring at the bottle.

What if the police find me? Charlie thought. What will they do to me at school? He wished Sammy were with him.

The old man looked in another trash can and found some pieces of broken tile. At another trash can he picked out a cookie cutter shaped like a heart. And so it went, from trash can to trash can, and from alley to alley, Charlie followed the old man as he collected dozens of discarded[1] pieces of once-useful things.

Charlie had never been in so many alleys before, or so far from home.

At last the wheelbarrow was full. The old man started off without stopping to check any more trash cans. He walked quickly, humming as he went.

Charlie was surprised at how fast the old man walked. He didn't know why anyone pushing such a load of junk would be singing . . . unless the old man really was crazy.

Down one street, around a corner, down another street, through traffic, across railroad tracks, Charlie followed the old man. He was in a neighborhood he'd never seen before. A police car went by. Charlie's breath caught in his chest as he ducked behind a telephone pole.

When he looked out from his hiding place, the police car was gone and so was the old man, who had disappeared around the corner. Charlie ran. He rushed around the corner. Crash! He ran right into the wheelbarrow, which tipped over with a bang. Junk flew everywhere, and Charlie fell to the sidewalk.

[1] thrown away; unwanted

"Why have you followed me?" demanded the old man, looking down at Charlie, and waving his hand.

"I-I-I didn't. You can't prove it," Charlie stammered, scrambling to his feet.

"All right," said the old man in a more gentle voice, and he bent over and began reloading the wheelbarrow. "I just thought you were following me and I wondered why."

Charlie saw that the old man wasn't going to hurt him, so he confessed. "I did follow you. I wanted to see where you take the junk you collect."

"Oh no, I can't let you find that out," said the old man.

"Why not?" asked Charlie.

"You're a crazy boy! You like busting and shooting and breaking everything. You might come and break my things."

"I don't care," answered Charlie, but he really did care, and he bent over and helped reload the wheelbarrow.

The old man was silent. They worked side by side until the wheelbarrow was full. Then he asked, "If I show you, will you promise never to come and break any of my things?"

"I-I-I promise," said Charlie, but he wasn't sure if he meant it.

"I'm Simon," said the old man softly.

"I'm Charlie."

The old man turned, bent over, took the handles of the wheelbarrow in his strong hands, and began to walk and hum. Charlie followed a few steps behind, wondering, 'Is he crazy? If he is, where is he leading me?'

They went a few more blocks and came to some railroad tracks. They crossed the tracks and then Charlie saw, rising high in the air, three tall, pointed towers. They looked like colorful fairy tale towers. He had never seen anything like them before.

The old man pushed his wheelbarrow along the strange wall that enclosed the towers. He unlocked a gate and went in. Charlie followed, his heart beating fast with fear and excitement.

Everywhere Charlie looked, there were strange structures made of cement and decorated with hundreds of pieces of tile, broken glass, parts of bottles, and whole seashells. And the cement itself had many designs cut into it. There were designs made by cookie cutters and by records and many other things Charlie recognized. It was a magic land. So many colors and circles and arches and shapes, and high above them all were the three tall towers.

"Do you see the junk?" the old man asked as he began unloading the wheelbarrow. "This is where I bring it."

"Here?" asked Charlie in disbelief. "No way. You don't bring it here. This place is cleaner than my house Saturday morning after we vacuum, sweep, and dust."

"I use it to build, to build the towers and all the things you see. I'm a poor man. I can't buy things to build with. So I build with things from trash cans, vacant lots, and junkyards. Things people think are no good. I make those things into something beautiful."

Charlie gazed about for a long time without saying anything. He didn't know what he expected when he followed the old man, but he certainly didn't expect this.

". . . I build with things from trash cans, vacant lots, and junkyards. Things people think are no good."

The old man smiled when he saw how excited Charlie was.

"You can look around," he said, "but remember your promise."

Charlie nodded and started off to explore.

The old man mixed some water, sand, and cement in a large bucket. He carried the heavy bucket, some broken tiles, and some bottle ends over to a corner. He smeared the wet cement on the wall. Then he pressed the bits of broken tile into the soft cement. Charlie came over and watched.

"Would you hand me those bottle ends?" asked the old man. "I'll put them here next to the tile."

Charlie handed him the bottle ends. He liked the flower the old man was making.

"Did you make all of this yourself?" he asked.

"All of it," said the old man. "I put in every stone, tile, bottle, shell, design, and shape . . . everything."

"Man!" declared Charlie. "You musta' worked a long time."

"More than thirty years," said the old man, and he smeared more fresh cement on the wall.

"How did you build those high towers?" Charlie asked.

"I made them strong with metal, wire, and cement. I climbed up, building as I climbed. Sometimes I took my lunch up with me."

"Can I climb them?" Charlie asked, eagerly looking up at the tallest tower.

"Go ahead. Use the ladders I built into the towers, and be careful," warned the old man.

So Charlie began to climb the highest tower. He wanted to go to the very top. But when he was about halfway up, he looked down. The ground was far below him. The old man looked very small. Charlie waved down at him, and he didn't climb any higher.

After Charlie climbed back down, he asked, "When you're finished, will you sell it?"

The old man laughed. "No, no, I didn't build this to sell."

"Then why'd you build it?"

"Because," began the old man. Then he paused. Slowly he looked all about him, at all the wonderful things he had made. "Because I wanted to build something beautiful."

Charlie wasn't sure he understood why someone would work for so long just to build something beautiful. But he was sure he liked what the old man had built.

"Can I play here again?" Charlie asked.

The old man smiled. "I'd like that."

"I could help you," said Charlie. "After school tomorrow, I'll bring some . . . some things from my alley."

"I thought I was almost finished," said the old man, "but with a strong boy like you to help me, I can build some more."

The old man looked at an empty spot along the wall.

"I've been wondering what to build there," he said.

"I know!" exclaimed Charlie, "we can build a wishing well."

"A wishing well. What a wonderful idea," said the old man.

"Only thing is," said Charlie, "I'm not exactly sure what a wishing well looks like."

"Like we want it to, Charlie! You bring your beautiful junk tomorrow. We'll build a wishing well together and we'll make it look just the way we want it to."

Postscript

The towers which Charlie discovered in the story actually exist. They can be seen in the Watts section of Los Angeles, California, where they were built by a man named Simon Rodia, who came to America from Italy.

Simon Rodia was a poor man who worked as a tile setter. He like to read about heroes like Marco Polo, Columbus, and Galileo. Once he said that a person has to do "good good or bad bad to be remembered." Maybe it was because Simon Rodia wanted to be remembered for doing something very good that he worked for thirty-three years to build the towers. Perhaps he also built the towers to remind him of similar towers in his native Italy. He often said the towers were a gift to his new country.

Simon Rodia worked all alone. He used only the simple tools of a tile setter and the belt and bucket of a window washer. For building materials, he collected more than seventy thousand seashells, dismantled[2] pipe structures and steel bedframes, and salvaged[3] countless tiles and bottles.

[2] took apart

[3] saved

In 1954, at the age of seventy-five, Simon Rodia completed his work, and he moved away. Many people thought he was a crazy man for building the towers. Children broke the tile and glass decorations. In 1957, Simon Rodia's house burned down. It seemed that his work was going to be destroyed and forgotten.

Some people realized how wonderful the towers were and wanted to save them. But the Los Angeles

[4] of poor quality

[5] mathematical figuring

City Building Department said that the towers must be destroyed because they were unsafe, having been built from junk and with inferior[4] construction methods.

A missile test engineer, using space-age calculations,[5] showed that though Simon Rodia had little book knowledge of the right way to build, his construction was safe. The building officials still were not satisfied. A pull test of the tallest tower was ordered. A cable was hooked from a truck to the top of the tallest tower. While television cameras turned and hundreds of people watched, the truck strained to pull the tower down. A shout of joy went up from the crowd. The tower stood firm. Only one seashell had fallen out of place.

Today, people come from all over the world to gaze and wonder at Simon Rodia's towers. Pictures of the towers appear in magazines from Tokyo to Paris. Simon Rodia's dream has come true. He is remembered for something "good good," something beautiful.

About the Author

Jon Madian says that he was "never very good in school." He was always in the lowest reading group and remembers being kept after school to learn to write his name. Today, in addition to writing books and poetry for young people, Mr. Madian, who lives in Oregon, runs his own software company.

Responding to the Story

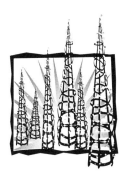

▼ **Think Back**

What does Charlie find strange about the old man?

Why is Charlie so interested in following the man?

How does Charlie's impression of Simon change?

▼ **Discuss**

Why does Simon show Charlie his creation after he has watched Charlie and his friend destroy things?

Simon doesn't want to sell his work. He only wants to build something beautiful. What other reasons might Simon Rodia have for building the towers?

Has this story changed the way you look at artwork or the artists who create it? If so, how?

▼ **Write**

Describe a Meeting To get readers to see Simon and Charlie as real people, author Jon Madian develops the characters by describing them and by telling what they say, do, or think. Write a short descriptive paragraph about the first time you met someone you now admire. Use the same techniques of characterization.

Write an Incident Have you ever known anyone who seems different from everyone else because he or she admires objects, music, or art that others find strange? Describe that person and write about an incident that reveals what he or she is like.

Theme Links

Accomplishments

In this unit, you've read about people who succeeded in accomplishing their dreams or goals. You have also thought about your own goals and about what it means to feel proud of something you've done.

▼ Group Discussion

With a partner or in a small group, talk about the selections in the unit and how they relate to the theme and to your own lives. Use questions like the following to guide the discussion.

• What is special about each character or subject?
• How did their accomplishments affect others?
• Which accomplishment can you relate to?
• How would you define an accomplishment?

▼ Meet the Characters

Imagine that you are a person or character from one of the selections in this unit. You've been asked to give a short speech about yourself—what you do, why you do it, and what it means to you. Write your speech, practice at home, and then give your speech to the class.

▼ Everyday Accomplishments

Start a scrapbook about people who have accomplished something important to them or to others. You can include people you know, people you have heard or read about, or yourself. Your scrapbook might include any of the following.

- newspaper or magazine clippings
- drawings
- photos
- charts, maps
- notes, letters

For each entry, write a paragraph or two describing the accomplishment and commenting on why you think it was worthwhile.

▼ The Theme and You

What is special about you? Think of something you've accomplished or would like to accomplish. Write a letter to a relative or friend sharing your news. Explain what it took to do what you did and how it made you feel. Or write about something you would like to do in the future and why you would like to do it.

Acts of Kindness

Acts of kindness—thoughtful things we do for one another—can be expressions of love, friendship, or even compassion. The way you treat other people and what you do for them can tell a lot about you.

The selections in this unit are about small and large acts of kindness. The ways the kindnesses are shown are as different as the people involved. As you read, think about the people in each of the readings. Imagine what motivated them to be so unselfish and how their kindness affected those around them.

Think about the kindest thing anyone ever did for you. What was it? What made it so special? How did you return the favor?

Oranges

Gary Soto

When two people understand each other, talking isn't always necessary. See how one lucky boy found that out.

The first time I walked
With a girl, I was twelve,
Cold, and weighted down
With two oranges in my jacket.
December. Frost cracking
Beneath my steps, my breath
Before me, then gone,
As I walked toward
Her house, the one whose
Porch light burned yellow
Night and day, in any weather.
A dog barked at me, until
She came out pulling
At her gloves, face bright
With rouge. I smiled,
Touched her shoulder, and led
Her down the street, across
A used car lot and a line
Of newly planted trees,

Until we were breathing
Before a drugstore. We
Entered, the tiny bell
Bringing a saleslady
Down a narrow aisle of goods.
I turned to the candies
Tiered[1] like bleachers,
And asked what she wanted—
Light in her eyes, a smile
Starting at the corners
Of her mouth. I fingered
A nickel in my pocket,
And when she lifted a chocolate
That cost a dime,
I didn't say anything.
I took the nickel from
My pocket, then an orange,
And set them quietly on
The counter. When I looked up,
The lady's eyes met mine,
And held them, knowing
Very well what it was all
About.

[1] set in rows

Outside,
A few cars hissing past,
Fog hanging like old
Coats between the trees.
I took my girl's hand
In mine for two blocks,
Then released it to let
Her unwrap the chocolate.
I peeled my orange
That was bright against
The gray of December
That, from some distance,
Someone might have thought
I was making a fire in my hands.

About the Author

Gary Soto was born in 1952 in Fresno, California. Many of his stories and poems are based on his memories of growing up in a close Mexican American family. His fiction includes *Baseball in April*, a collection of short stories, *Taking Sides, Pacific Crossing,* and *Local News.* He also has produced two short films—*The Pool Party* and *A Summer Life.*

Responding to the Poem

▼ Think Back

How does the speaker feel about the girl? How can you tell?

How does the speaker pay for the chocolate?

What kind thing does the lady in the store do?

▼ Discuss

Why didn't the speaker say anything when the girl picked candy that cost a dime, even though he only had a nickel? What would you have done?

The speaker says "When I looked up,/The lady's eyes met mine,/And held them, knowing/Very well what it was all/About." What was it all/About?

▼ Write

Create Similes A simile uses the words *like* or *as* to compare two unlike things. Note Soto's simile for fog.

   Fog hanging like old/Coats between the trees.

Think of interesting comparisons for other elements of weather, such as rain, snow, mist, and wind. Write three or four similes.

Tell Your Diary Do you remember your first date? What was it like? Write a poem or diary entry that describes what you did on your first date and how you felt. Use similes to add interest to your writing.

Andrew

Berry Morgan

Have you ever had to make sacrifices for the people you love? If so, you will understand the feelings of Roxie, the woman in this story. Roxie's way of speaking reflects where she lives—the rural South. As you read, notice the details that tell you what her life has been like. Why does Roxie want to help other people?

[1] aid in the nesting and hatching of eggs

Roxie Stoner lives in rural Mississippi. Since her mother died, Roxie is very lonely. One day she takes someone's baby home to care for it. Even though Roxie means well, she gets into trouble.

There was only one time in my life I had a little baby off all to myself. No kin, that is. I used to love to have my brother that drives the pulp truck bring *his*, but Mama couldn't stand too much of their commotion and they gave her colds with their everlasting sneezes till we had to wean him from it, and they grew up hardly ever stopping.

This all began with that white lady that calls me every year along in the spring to help her set[1] her ducks. I've fooled with ducks so long now it looks like they will go on and do anything I want them to, and it has spread around the country so that I have calls for it just like a doctor. Well, it's uphill all the way from my house to this lady's house, and I was taking it nice and slow and stopping to rest every now and then and look around. I had got as far as the bluff by the corner of the old Somerset place and just looked up—I always get plums from those particular trees since nobody else seems to know about them—and lo and behold, what do I see sitting on the gallery[2] of that old tumbled down cabin but a young girl. Her legs were hanging loose over the edge and she was swinging them back and forth and looking down at the road where I was standing. Do I know her, I thought—because I *do* know nearly everybody in King County. She might have come up from Bogue, though, and Mama always said to stay out of the way of Bogue, white *or* colored, and I have, but no, if I wasn't telling myself wrong, this was one of old lady Littell's grandchildren that they've kept sending her back from Chicago and all around for years and years.

[2] porch

"Are you all right, honey?" I asked her. "What are you doing way out here by yourself?"

I was sorry for saying that, because just about then I saw *him*—or anyhow an undershirt showing up white at the door. So she must be married, and that was why she was out here away from school and her grandmother in this old empty cabin.

"Yes ma'am," she said, taking time to smile with me and act sweet. "How are you, Miss Roxie?"

So she knew me. Before I could answer, I heard it—a little high crying noise behind her in the cabin. Right away I knew what had made it. They had a baby up in there, their own little baby, and most likely they were out here tending to it because back in town he had another rightful wife who would catch him and get him back. But where was their water, poor things, what did they do for water? The place didn't have enough roof left to catch any even if they had a gutter, which I disbelieved.

The gentleman must have picked it up, because the crying stopped. I knew I had to some way or other get up on that bluff and hold that little thing myself. "I don't have time right now," I told the girl, "but when I come back from setting a duck could I please see the baby? What is its name?"

She smiled and nodded her head to show manners. "Yes ma'am," she said, "you'd be welcome. Andrew. His name is Andrew."

Well, I went on up the hill to do what I'd said I'd do, and it took nearly all day. This white lady had saved up a winter's talk—wanted to tell me her frights since last spring, has two worrisome boys that she is afraid may drink a little beer. By the time I petted the duck and got it started on its eggs, she had gone on and fixed me a plate of dinner to eat on the back steps so she could talk some more.

The sun was halfway down the woods when I got back to where the cabin was, and reddening up to set because it was March and still cool. I didn't hear anything now except the birds, and I couldn't see any footholds on the outside of the cliff to climb up by. It looked a whole lot different than it had in the morning—long shadows everywhere to make me wonder if they were still up there with it.

It came into my head to give up—Mama always did hate to have me prowling too close to dark. Still I had said I was coming and they might be expecting me. Just then as the good Lord *would* have it, I caught the scent of woodsmoke. So they were still up there and even had themselves a fire. "Hello" I said every once in a while, but my voice doesn't carry and I didn't hear anything back. Just when I got to the top, though, I saw her, standing in the door with a frying pan in her hand—fixing to clean it out, I reckon, because she stooped down to a pile of moss and sticks on the gallery floor.

"How is it?" I asked her. "Is it resting well?"

"Yes ma'am," she said, knocking the frying pan on the gallery edge to clear it. "It seems like it is."

"That's good," I said. "How old is it? How long ago did you find little Andrew?"

I was afraid this had really hurt her feelings, but after a while she told me. "About a week. It's been just about a week."

"Do you have any milk to nurse it with?"

She shook her head. "It haven't come in yet."

"Well," I said, "that's what I was afraid of. It's got to have its milk, and like Mama used to say, not tomorrow or the next day but right now." I was on the gallery myself by this time, and nearly every board I set my foot on came up at the other end—loose. She tried to watch out for me that I didn't go through until she could push the old door back—it was off its hinges—to make room for me to pass. Right away I saw those foolish children had made a fire in the middle of the

Andrew **51**

floor, just on a piece of roof tin—didn't have sense enough to build it in the fireplace. "Sweet girl," I said, "you're fixing to burn this old place down." And I reached and picked up a piece of rag and took the tin by the corner to pull it onto the hearth.[3] As soon as I straightened up, she took me over to the baby. It was in an old cardboard box, and she had put all the soft things she had under it. It was sound asleep, a precious little boy baby a dark beautiful brown about the same shade, if I reckoned correctly, as Mama. "This is in God's image," I told the girl. "A sign of his love and a brand new life to be used for his glorification. Where's its papa?"

[3] fireplace floor

"He's about gone to get milk," the girl answered. "Leastways that's what I told him to do."

"Does he have any money?"

She bent over the box and looked hard at the baby. Oh, she was proud. You could see that. "He say he have."

I knew Mama wouldn't like me doing this but I couldn't help it. "My house is nice and warm and I have a can of Pet[4] we can put some boiled water with and give it by an eyedropper, just a little at a time until it builds its strength. Come on with me and we will leave *him* a note if you have anything to write on."

[4] a brand of canned milk

She was still smiling all right enough, but she shook her pretty head. "He told me to stay on right here, Miss Roxie, not to leave."

"Is this a King's Town man?"

"No ma'am," she said. "It's a United States soldier."

Just drifting through then, I thought, and apt to drift on. "Well, we've got to give it milk. If you have to wait for the soldier, go ahead and wait, but let me take it on, wrap it in this fresh apron and carry it home. When it's good and strong, you can come and get it."

———————

I had wrapped the
baby up the best
I could, and I kissed its
mother and gave her the
fifty cents I'd made from
setting the duck.

———————

She leaned over the baby and looked at it again, like it might get up out of its sleep and tell her what to do.

"It's near dark," I said. "You go on and wait if you have to, but I've got to get this baby its supper. And you really ought to go with me and fix yourself up for tomorrow's school—learn something, and not stay out here in these woods with a United States soldier or anybody else." I had wrapped the baby up the best I could, and I kissed its mother and gave her the fifty cents I'd made from setting the duck. Then I was afraid of falling, going down the bluff with it, but by sitting down and sliding on a little at a time I was right down in the road and it was safe.

As soon as I started walking, I began to be happy. This was a real living baby I had to myself—God's image, like I had known it was in the cabin. "If it please Thee," I said, "let this little baby—Andrew is its name—grow strong and tall and take up Thy war against evil." It hardly weighed anything at all.

There is such a change in a house when you first take a baby into it. I put him down on Mama's bed—the first person ever laid there since the evening she passed. "Well sir, Andrew," I said, "there's so much to do and only you and me to do it, I wonder where to start." I could rock it after I put on the water—that would take a while to heat and then cool. By the time I did this, it had its eyes open and was twisting its head a whole lot, like it already knew it had changed its resting place. "Eating is the main thing," I said to it. "After you've had a few drops of weak Pet you'll sleep, and after you sleep I'll strengthen the Pet just enough to make you sleep some more. And all that time you'll be growing and getting bigger. By the time I have to give you back, you'll be looking around here like the Lord of creation—might even have caught on how to smile." If they let me keep him long enough, I could even make him apt[5] in his books, and it made me want to cry to think of him starting to school, getting on the bus and riding off.

Andrew liked rocking. Then after I had given him the first Pet with Mama's eyedropper, I heated a sheet and wrapped his stomach good and rocked some more. He didn't cry at all except when he woke up and wanted more milk. "You are going to keep Roxie up all

[5] smart

night," I told him, "but that's all right. When Mama was here, I never was able to sleep more than an hour at a time without her needing something, and now God has sent me a precious lamb in her place."

I would sleep and it would sleep. It felt so good to know it was lying there by me in the dark. I wished it hadn't been given a name yet, because I might name it for Mama's father, the Reverend Isaac Stoner. But you don't hear the name Isaac much anymore and I guess Andrew *was* better.

Along toward morning, even before the mill whistle, I thought I heard a car on our creek road. Who could that be, I thought. They wouldn't come for it before daylight, and besides that the girl and the United States soldier didn't have a car, and whoever this was did. When I heard it drawing up into our yard, I got up and found my wrapper.[6] I braced the baby—it was too little to roll, but still it looked safer with something between it and the edge—and by that time there was knocking on my door.

It was Mr. Bat Becker, the sheriff's helper, and old lady Littell herself, as vexed[7] as she could be.

"I hate to disturb you this time of night," Mr. Bat said, "but there's this little baby missing, and Eliza here's granddaughter says you're the one harboring it."

Well, I took them right in to show them it was safe and happy. But instead of being glad and taking my word, Mrs. Littell, poor old worn-out soul, snatched it off the bed and began looking at every part of it to see if it was true. Then she held it tight and began to moan

[6] shawl

[7] angry

and cry and kiss it so hard you wouldn't believe she already had a house full of them, all different sizes.

[8] mentally slow

"Mrs. Stoner always did say you were backward,"[8] she told me, "but she didn't let on you were a thief." I felt bad to hear her talk like that, but she was so old and worked up—had been afraid, I guess, that it was thrown back in the woods to buzzards—she couldn't help it. I begged her pardon over and over, and they went on out and slammed the door.

[9] Piggly Wiggly, a grocery store

Oh, yes, I see him now and then. Twice I caught up with him at the Piggly[9] and once at the oil station, where they have a Coke machine. And he *is* fine. I give him a nickel if I have one, and he always has a big smile for me—thank you ma'am, no idea in the world who I really am. That's all right, Andrew, I say (just to myself), because I had you for one night, you lying up there in my lap taking milk, and if I'm any judge at all of what is true, you loved me.

About the Author

Berry Morgan won a Houghton Mifflin Literary Fellowship in 1966 for a series of books about rural life in Mississippi. "Andrew" is an excerpt from *The Mystic Adventures of Roxie Stoner,* the second in the series. Morgan also has written for the *New Yorker* magazine.

Responding to the Story

▼ Think Back

Where is Roxie going when she first meets Andrew and his mother? Why is she going there?

Who are Andrew's parents?

What makes Roxie think that Andrew's mother can't take care of him?

▼ Discuss

Roxie says she wanted to give Andrew food and a warm place to live. She also seems to have personal reasons for wanting him to live with her. What are they?

Mrs. Littell, Andrew's great-grandmother, says that Roxie is "backward." She also seems to think that Roxie might have hurt the baby. What do you think? Would Roxie make a good mother? Why or why not?

▼ Write

Point of View Because the story is told from Roxie's point of view, you see events as Roxie sees them and feel empathy for her. Suppose Mrs. Littell were telling the story. Write a brief description of Roxie from Mrs. Littell's point of view.

As Andrew Sees It What if Andrew was able to describe what was happening to him? How would he describe his parents? His grandmother? Roxie? Rewrite the story from Andrew's point of view and discuss with a classmate how it is different from Roxie's story.

Thank You, M'am

Langston Hughes

A lady's purse was too tempting for one boy to ignore. Find out why he was lucky that he chose Mrs. Jones to rob.

She was a large woman with a large purse that had everything in it but a hammer and nails. It had a long strap, and she carried it slung across her shoulder. It was about eleven o'clock at night, dark, and she was walking alone, when a boy ran up behind her and tried to snatch her purse. The strap broke with the sudden single tug the boy gave it from behind. But the boy's weight and the weight of the purse combined caused him to lose his balance. Instead of taking off full blast as he had hoped, the boy fell on his back on the sidewalk and his legs flew up. The large woman simply turned around and kicked him right square in his blue-jeaned sitter. Then she reached down, picked the boy up by his shirt front, and shook him until his teeth rattled.

After that the woman said, "Pick up my pocketbook, boy, and give it here."

She still held him tightly. But she bent down enough to permit him to stoop and pick up her purse. Then she said, "Now ain't you ashamed of yourself?"

Firmly gripped by his shirt front, the boy said, "Yes'm."

The woman said, "What did you want to do it for?"

The boy said, "I didn't aim to."

She said, "You a lie!"

By that time two or three people passed, stopped, turned to look, and some stood watching.

"If I turn you loose, will you run?" asked the woman.

"Yes'm," said the boy.

"Then I won't turn you loose," said the woman. She did not release him.

"Lady, I'm sorry," whispered the boy.

"Um-hum! Your face is dirty. I got a great mind to wash your face for you. Ain't you got nobody home to tell you to wash your face?"

"No'm," said the boy.

"Then it will get washed this evening," said the large woman, starting up the street, dragging the frightened boy behind her.

He looked as if he were fourteen or fifteen, frail and willow-wild, in tennis shoes and blue jeans.

The woman said, "You ought to be my son. I would teach you right from wrong. Least I can do right now is to wash your face. Are you hungry?"

"No'm," said the being-dragged boy. "I just want you to turn me loose."

"Was I bothering *you* when I turned that corner?" asked the woman.

"No'm."

"But you put yourself in contact with *me*," said the woman. "If you think that contact is not going to last awhile, you got another thought coming. When I get through with you, sir, you are going to remember Mrs. Luella Bates Washington Jones."

Sweat popped out on the boy's face and he began to struggle. Mrs. Jones stopped, jerked him around in front of her, put a half nelson[1] about his neck, and continued to drag him up the street. When she got to her door, she dragged the boy inside, down a hall, and into a large kitchenette-furnished room at the rear of the house. She switched on the light and left the door open. The boy could hear other roomers laughing and talking in the large house. Some of their doors were open, too, so he knew he and the woman were not alone. The woman still had him by the neck in the middle of her room.

She said, "What is your name?"

"Roger," answered the boy.

"Then, Roger, you go to that sink and wash your face," said the woman, whereupon she turned him loose—at last. Roger looked at the door—looked at the woman—looked at the door—*and went to the sink.*

"Let the water run till it gets warm," she said. "Here's a clean towel."

"You gonna take me to jail?" asked the boy, bending over the sink.

"Not with that face, I would not take you nowhere," said the woman. "Here I am trying to get

[1] a wrestling hold

home to cook me a bite to eat, and you snatch my pocketbook! Maybe you ain't been to your supper either, late as it be. Have you?"

"There's nobody home at my house," said the boy.

"Then we'll eat," said the woman. "I believe you're hungry—or been hungry—to try to snatch my pocketbook!"

"I want a pair of blue suede shoes," said the boy.

"Well, you didn't have to snatch *my* pocketbook to get some suede shoes," said Mrs. Luella Bates Washington Jones. "You could of asked me."

"Ma'am?"

The water dripping from his face, the boy looked at her. There was a long pause. A very long pause. After he had dried his face, and not knowing what else to do, dried it again, the boy turned around, wondering what next. The door was open. He could make a dash for it down the hall. He could run, run, run, *run!*

The woman was sitting on the daybed. After a while she said, "I were young once and I wanted things I could not get."

There was another long pause. The boy's mouth opened. Then he frowned, not knowing he frowned.

The woman said, "Um-humm! You thought I was going to say *but*, didn't you? You thought I was going to say, *but I didn't snatch people's pocketbooks.* Well, I wasn't going to say that." Pause. Silence. "I have done things, too, which I would not tell you, son—neither tell God, if He didn't already know. Everybody's got something in common, so you set down while I fix us something to eat. You might run that comb through your hair so you will look presentable."

In another corner of the room behind a screen was a gas plate and an icebox. Mrs. Jones got up and went behind the screen. The woman did not watch the boy to see if he was going to run now, nor did she watch her purse, which she left behind her on the daybed. But the boy took care to sit on the far side of the room, away from the purse, where he thought she could easily see him out of the corner of her eye if she wanted to. He did not trust the woman *not* to trust him. And he did not want to be mistrusted now.

"Do you need somebody to go to the store," asked the boy, "maybe to get some milk or something?"

"Don't believe I do," said the woman, "unless you just want sweet milk yourself. I was going to make cocoa out of this canned milk I got here."

"That will be fine," said the boy.

She heated some lima beans and ham she had in the icebox, made the cocoa, and set the table. The woman did not ask the boy anything about where he lived, or his folks, or anything else that would embarrass him. Instead, as they ate, she told him about her job in a hotel beauty shop that stayed open late, what the work was like, and how all kinds of women came in and out, blondes, redheads, and Spanish. Then she cut him a half of her ten-cent cake.

"Eat some more, son," she said.

When they were finished eating, she got up and said, "Now here, take this ten dollars and buy yourself some blue suede shoes. And next time, do not make the mistake of latching onto *my* pocketbook *nor nobody else's*—because shoes got by devilish ways will burn your feet. I got to get my rest now. But from here on in, son, I hope you will behave yourself."

She led him down the hall to the front door and opened it. "Good night! Behave yourself, boy!" she said, looking out into the street as he went down the steps.

The boy wanted to say something other than, "Thank you, m'am," to Mrs. Luella Bates Washington Jones, but although his lips moved, he couldn't even say that as he turned at the foot of the barren stoop[2] and looked up at the large woman in the door. Then she shut the door.

[2] a small, open porch at the front of a house

About the Author

Langston Hughes (1902–1967) was born in Joplin, Missouri. He wrote poems, short stories, novels, and plays. He also achieved success as a songwriter and lecturer. Hughes traveled all over the world and based many of his writings on his experiences and on what it meant to be an African-American in his time.

Responding to the Story

▼ Think Back

Is Mrs. Luella Jones afraid of the young thief? What details give you clues about how she feels?

What was Roger going to buy with the stolen money?

How does Luella Jones treat Roger? How does she feel about him? How can you tell?

▼ Discuss

What do you think motivated Luella Jones to take Roger home, clean and feed him, and then give him ten dollars?

Do you think Roger will go back to stealing pocket-books in the future? Why or why not? Do you think this incident will change Roger's life? What is Langston Hughes's message in the story? Explain.

▼ Write

Write an Explanation Since "Thank You, M'am" is told from Roger's point of view, it is only through dialogue that readers can understand what Luella Jones is like. Skim the story for dialogue that reveals Mrs. Jones's personality. Briefly write what each passage reveals.

Update the Story Rewrite a scene from "Thank You, M'am" as it might happen today. You can use the same characters or create new ones. Use dialogue that sounds the way people really talk.

Coming Home: A Dog's True Story

Ted Harriott

y first master was an old man called Paddy. He had a smoky smell about him as if he had sat hunched over a fire for years.

The floorboards in our room were hard and splintery but I was not allowed on the chairs or the bed. He was strict about the rules, but he was kind to me. He fed me most days and only shouted when I got something wrong.

He called me Bodger and we spent the days walking the streets. I had to stay close to him, though he walked even more slowly than most humans.

Paddy gave me two important jobs. The first was to beg for food in the shops. The second was to sniff out things in the dustbins.[1] When I found something, Paddy called me good boy and scratched my ears.

Sometimes, after we had eaten, Paddy would say in his happy voice, "Come on then, my old Bodger. Let's go up the pub[2] and have a drink." There were always other people at the pub, drinking from pint mugs and

Do you ever wonder what animals would say if they could talk? In this story, you'll find out what one dog has on his mind.

[1] garbage cans

[2] a place that serves food and liquor

laughing loudly. Paddy told them stories about the old days and they said, "Have another one, Paddy." I did tricks for them and they gave me pieces of pie and sausage.

Paddy and I would go home late on those special nights.

But, one winter, Paddy suddenly became tired and didn't want to go for walks with me any more.

I saw that he was frightened when a young woman came to our room and told him, "You will have to go into hospital for a long time. We'll have your old dog taken care of."

"Taken care of!" shouted Paddy. "Put down, you mean."

Paddy was trembling when the woman left. He pulled me on to his bed and held me in his arms— something he had never done before. I was worried. I wasn't allowed on the bed.

Then he got up, closed the door and started piling things against it. I whined because he was so upset. I tried to tell him that soon it would be spring again, but he wouldn't listen. He just lay down and went to sleep.

Next morning when I woke up I tried to get Paddy out of bed to open the door for me. He just patted my head. I was hungry and thirsty, but I soon found out how to lap a little water from the dripping tap over the sink.

I was pleased with my discovery and ran to tell Paddy so that he could get some. I nosed his ear. It was cold and he did not move. He had gone away somewhere and I knew he would never come back.

I howled and howled, but no one came for days. At last, policemen smashed down the door. I was so weak that I could only just get up to wag my tail and greet them.

They took me to a place called the Dogs' Home and locked me in a cage with a stone floor. There were rows of cages full of dogs. It was such a sad place. We all knew that if we were not rescued soon we would be taken through the door at the end of the corridor. Dogs never came back from there.

I would surely go through that door. Who would want me now? I was all skin and bones, and had lost a lot of hair.

After a few days I watched a woman walk along the corridor. The other dogs all called out to her, "Take me! Take me!" But she came straight to my cage. And then I recognized her. She was one of the people Paddy and I used to see on our walks. The attendant opened the cage door—I was saved!

For the next few hours I wasn't sure that I liked being saved. The woman took me first to a man she called the vet, who stuck a needle into me, bathed and powdered me.

They were getting me ready for someone to see me.

I began to understand what it was all about when she told the vet, "I don't know what I'll do if he says I can't keep the dog."

Then she took me to her home, where we sat and waited. At last a man arrived. He stared hard at me and I held my breath. He *had* to let me stay. I lay under the table peeping out. I couldn't take my eyes off him as the woman told him about me. I hoped he understood how frightened I was that I might be sent back to the Dogs' Home.

"Can we keep him?" asked the woman.

It seemed a long time before he answered, "All right. We'll see how it goes."

I wriggled out of my hiding place and he held his hand out to me. I sniffed it and then licked it gently. He was my new master. But I wondered if he could ever love me as much as Paddy had.

Then I had an idea. I asked if I could go out and my mistress opened the door for me. I hunted about and my nose led me to a metal dustbin. The smell was strong and exciting. I reached in and took something out.

I hurried upstairs again and scratched at the door. When my master opened it, I wagged my tail and dropped my gift at his feet.

"He's brought us a present," said my new mistress as she hugged me.

"A smelly old lump of cheese," said my master. He was smiling and he patted me, running his hands along my sides. "He's very thin and his skin's in a bad state," he said. "He's been through rough times but he'll be all right now."

He thought for a minute . . . "Let's call him Job."

Responding to the Story

▼ Think Back

What was Bodger's first master like? List some details that give you clues about him.

What does Bodger think of his new master?

What acts of kindness are described in "Coming Home"?

▼ Discuss

Why do you think the woman wanted to take in Bodger? What would you have done?

Many people argue that humans are often kinder to animals than they are to other people. Do you agree? Why or why not?

▼ Write

Write an Explanation Do you think that because "Coming Home" is told from the dog's point of view, readers feel more empathy for Bodger? Why or why not? Write a paragraph or two explaining why you think Ted Harriott wrote the story from the dog's perspective.

Read Her Thoughts Imagine that the woman who adopts Bodger tells the story. How would the ending be different? Write a short monologue revealing what the woman is thinking when she rescues Bodger from the dog shelter.

Birdfoot's Grampa

Joseph Bruchac

To one old man, saving toads is as important as saving people. How would you describe this kind of person?

The old man

must have stopped our car

two dozen times to climb out

and gather into his hands

the small toads blinded

by our lights and leaping,

live drops of rain.

The rain was falling,

a mist about his white hair

and I kept saying

you can't save them all

accept it, get back in

we've got places to go.

But, leathery hands full

of wet brown life

knee deep in the summer

roadside grass,

he just smiled and said

they have places to go to

too

About the Author

Joseph Bruchac is a storyteller, poet, and editor. His poems and stories have appeared in more than 400 magazines and anthologies. Bruchac's experiences include teaching creative writing and African literature in Ghana. He takes pride in tracing part of his ancestry to the Abenaki group of Native Americans and has written autobiographical pieces about that. He also has translated numerous Native American and West African works into English.

Responding to the Poem

▼ Think Back

What does the old man try to do?

How does the speaker rationalize not stopping the car?

What is the old man like? What details give you clues about him?

▼ Discuss

Have you ever seen animals on a busy street or highway? What have you done in those situations? What should you do?

What does the old man mean when he says that the toads have places to go to too?

▼ Write

Vivid Images Joseph Bruchac uses vivid images to describe a rainy summer night along the roadside. Skim "Birdfoot's Grampa." List the words and phrases that create powerful and memorable images.

Create a Scene Think about a situation in which you helped an animal. What images come to mind? List some images that describe the time and place. You might use those images in a poem about the incident.

Grandma Hattie

Tom Bodett

G oing through the Christmas cards in our mailbox today, I came across one from my dear old grandma in Illinois. She never fails. Never missed a birthday, Christmas, or anniversary as long as I've lived. Quite a gal, old Grandma Hattie. There's always a nice little letter inside wrapped around a crisp five-dollar bill she can't afford to send.

I read the letter—newsy stuff about her holiday baking and the weather (no snow there yet either). Then as always, there was the postscript at the end: "Just a little Christmas treat. Love, Grandma." So I tucked the five-dollar bill into my shirt and promised that my wife and I would do something extra-special with it. At least as special as five bucks will buy you these days.

Then, as I was reading through the rest of the mail, I came across another card from Grandma. I'll be darned. Must be our anniversary card, being as we were married the day after Christmas, same as her birthday. She never forgets. I was wrong. It was another

Maybe you know somebody like Grandma Hattie. What makes that person so special?

Christmas card with another newsy little letter and another brand-new five-dollar bill she couldn't afford to send. Well, what do you think of that?

She must have got confused somehow and forgot to cross us off her list. Or maybe she doesn't have a list. She may do it from memory, and eighty-seven-year-old memories can play tricks like that at times. She may have thought she already sent us one but wasn't altogether sure, so she sent another one just in case. That would be just like her. Rather than take the chance of missing one of us by mistake, she'd send two just to be sure. There aren't many of us that can afford the five dollars that would do that. The heck of it is that I don't dare send it back. She'd be so embarrassed by the mistake, it would do her no good, and I'm sure we can get it back to her in other ways.

There's probably not a whole lot of Christmases left in Grandma Hat, and the world will be the worse for it when she goes. She's endeared herself to friends, family, and strangers alike for many, many decades. My mom tells a story of her from the Depression[1] years.

At the time, Grandma and Grandpa owned a dairy. It was right next door to the house, where the garden is now, and they ran it themselves. They lived near the train tracks, and being that it was during the Depression, they used to get their share of hoboes[2] coming around looking for handouts.

They were hard-working folks, my mom's family, and believed that everybody else should be too. They'd give the "bums," as she called them, food and milk, all

[1] a period in history from 1929–1939 when businesses failed and many people couldn't find work

[2] old-fashioned term for homeless people who travel from place to place

right. But they'd have to wash milk cans, scrub floors, shovel snow, or some such thing to get it. Those were the rules, and nobody complained.

Mom says they got pretty popular on the hobo circuit and got that inevitable[3] mark on their front gatepost. Just a little X on the post in white chalk to let the other hoboes know this was a place where a guy could get a handout. It was common practice at that time and was supposed to be on the sly.[4] But Grandma knew it was there. She never did bother any with that chalk on the gatepost, except just once.

It was Christmastime, and my mom was just a little girl. They didn't have any snow yet, but right before Christmas they had a big wind and rain storm. Coming back from church that Sunday, Grandma noticed that the chalk mark had been washed clear off the post by the storm.

It got cold right away like it will on the midwestern plains, and snowed to beat the band.[5] She sat that day in the front room saying the rosary with Grandpa like they always did on Sunday. They saw the hoboes walking down from the train yard going wherever it is hoboes go in a snowstorm. They looked so cold and defeated, but none of them was stopping at the gate or knocking on the dairy window like they always did. Then it struck her why. Of course—the little white X wasn't on the post anymore. Now, where another person might have been relieved to be left alone the Sunday before Christmas, Old Grandma Hat, and she wasn't that old then, put on her overcoat, went right out

[3] sure to happen

[4] secret

[5] very heavily

to the gatepost, and put a great big white X there where nobody could miss it.

I don't know if they got to feed any hoboes that day or not because Mom usually stops telling the story about there, but it doesn't matter. It told me something about Grandma, and I've carried this story with me a long time. She put that X on the gatepost way back then for the same reason she sent us two Christmas cards this year. She didn't want to miss anybody, even if it did cost an extra five bucks. I always think of that story when I'm starting to feel a little broke and put out at Christmas; then I'm ashamed of myself.

So I don't know what all this means except that in this hard-hearted world we live in, we should all have a gatepost out front, and at least for this one time of year let's all go out and put a great big white X on that thing.

About the Author

Tom Bodett was born in 1955 in Champaign, Illinois. He worked as a logger, construction worker, and commercial fisherman before he achieved success as a writer. His folksy style of writing and speaking has made him a popular columnist for the *Anchorage Daily News* and a commentator for public radio. "Grandma Hattie" is from *As Far As You Can Go Without a Passport,* a collection of his comments and comic pieces.

Responding to the Essay

▼ Think Back

What acts of kindness are described in "Grandma Hattie"?

What kinds of letters does Grandma Hattie send?

Why doesn't Tom Bodett want to send the second five-dollar bill back to Grandma Hattie?

▼ Discuss

Bodett says that they can get the second five dollars back to Grandma Hattie in other ways. How might Bodett return Grandma Hattie's generosity?

Why did Grandma Hattie go out in the storm to put the white X back on the gatepost? What do you think happened after she did that?

▼ Write

Keep a Journal An anecdote is a story within a story, a short passage that illustrates a point or tells what a character or person is like. How does Tom Bodett introduce his anecdote about Grandma Hattie? What is the purpose of the anecdote? In your journal or portfolio, start listing some incidents that you could turn into anecdotes. Share your list with a partner.

Write an Anecdote Do you have a story to tell about someone? Using "Grandma Hattie" as a model, write an anecdote illustrating what that person is like.

Theme Links

Acts of Kindness

In this unit, you've read about people who acted out of kindness to help others. You have discussed what motivates people to be kind and thought about how your own acts of kindness make you feel.

▼ Group Discussion

In a small group, talk about the various people and acts of kindness you read about in this unit. Use questions like the following to guide your discussion.

- In what ways were people kind to one another? How were they kind to animals?
- Which act of kindness was particularly thoughtful?
- Which character was most like you? How?

▼ Hearing from the Characters

Imagine you are a person from a selection in this unit, either the person who performed the act of kindness or the one who received it. As a guest on a TV talk show, you are asked to talk about how acts of kindness can change a person's life. Prepare by taking notes about how giving or receiving kindness affected you. Why did you do what you did? How did the act change your life? What would you say to the other person involved? Work with a partner, switching the roles of talk show host and guest. If possible, videotape your talk.

▼ Everyday Acts of Kindness

With a group, create an award for individuals who have performed acts of kindness. Learn about people in your school or community who have acted unselfishly to help others. Since your goal in this unit was to explore many types of kindness, plan on giving out a number of awards.

- Create and duplicate a plaque, medal, or certificate to symbolize the award.
- Talk to fellow students, your parents, teachers, and others to get a list of recipients. For each recipient, write a short description of why they should receive the award.
- Present the individuals with the awards.

▼ The Theme and You

Have you performed any acts of kindness that you are proud of, or has someone done something special for you? Is there something you'd like to do for someone? Write a thank you card to a person who did a favor for you. Tell how the favor made you feel and how it helped you. If you plan on doing a favor for someone, write a note describing what you plan to do and why.

Communication

You, like most people, probably enjoy sharing ideas and information with others. How do you do this? When do you talk with people face to face? Do you like to talk on the telephone? Do you write letters to relatives and friends to share news?

Communicating is not always easy or successful. Have there ever been times when you just couldn't explain your ideas or get people to understand you? Some selections in this unit show people struggling to communicate. The people face many barriers—physical challenges, long-distance relationships, or misunderstandings. All the readings, however, illustrate how important communication is.

As you read, think about what it would be like if you could not share your ideas and feelings. Then imagine yourself in the place of the characters in the selections. Ask yourself what you would have done in each situation.

Letter for Sookan

Sook Nyul Choi

Sookan Bak came from Korea to attend college in the United States. Her days are so busy, Sookan hardly has time to write home. Her mother's first letter arrives.

What would it be like to leave your home and family and everything familiar to go to college in another country halfway around the world? Why would it be important to keep in touch?

I stared at the unopened letter from Mother. It felt strange to see my own handwriting on the envelope. The night before I left Seoul, I had stayed up all night attending to last-minute details. One of these was to stamp and address twenty envelopes to myself. Mother did not know English, and I wanted her to feel free to write me without having to ask my brothers to address the envelopes for her. I knew how Mother hated imposing[1] on her children. She always said that young people have their own worries, and that her job was to see that her children had the time to live their own lives.

She was very different from the other mothers I knew. She never talked of filial[2] duty, of the obligations[3] we had to our elders and our ancestors. One of Mother's

[1] taking advantage of

[2] family

[3] things that one must do

favorite sayings was "Just as water runs down, so does love." She felt responsible for setting a good example, and just as she loved us, she expected us to love each other, and our children.

She never complained about her hardships, and instead said, "One cannot live looking up. One must look down to those less fortunate and must help them. One has to appreciate what one has in life." With Father gone, she struggled to make ends meet with the little money my brothers were able to earn. And yet, she was always there to help those less fortunate.

This flood of memories overwhelmed me. I longed for my mother. I missed her quiet smile that always seemed to fill me with strength. I felt guilty that I was not by her side. I slowly opened her letter.

Dear Sookan,

It is midnight. Even your ducks are asleep by the pond. They are big now, perhaps a little too big for our small pond. They waddle all around the yard, and sometimes follow me all the way to the street. I can hear your brothers snoring. They fall asleep so quickly; it is the gift of youth.

I am wearing the sweater you insisted on finishing before you left. How stubborn you were to stay up all night before that long trip. But I do love it, and wear it all the time. It keeps me warm on nights like tonight. The cool weather seems to be setting in already, and in the evening, it is quite chilly here. I wonder if we packed enough clothes for you and if you are warm enough in America.

I was in the greenhouse earlier, checking on my chrysanthemums. They will be fluffy and beautiful this season. When they are in full bloom, I will cut some to give to Father Lee for Sunday service. My contribution each Sunday is so small that I thought of supplementing it with my flowers. It will make me feel that I support my church.

Your older brothers like to wear the thin cotton socks you knit before you left. Inchun pulled out the vest you made, and wore it yesterday. I think he was glad the weather became cool enough for it. He looks so handsome in the vest; the light gray color you chose suits him so well. It was a good thing you learned how to knit as that is one of the things I never learned.

We all miss you. The house feels empty without you.

I read your postcards as soon as our good mailman brings them. He is getting old now, and has been having more and more trouble with his legs this year. But he knows how important your letters are, and always brings them all the way up to the house for me. I am so grateful to him that I offer him a cup of tea every time he comes. He asked me to say hello to you for him.

In the evening, when we are all together, we read your postcards aloud. I am sorry we are not sending you any money. What little you had with you must have been gone long ago. I think your brothers do not write because they have no money to send you. Forgive this helpless mother who sends her daughter so far away and cannot even mail a little pocket money each month.

I am glad you like your new friends and college in America. It must be hard to adjust to the new culture and the new way of doing things. The language alone must cause you problems. Although you sound so cheerful and happy, I can imagine the difficulties you face. I will never know exactly what they are, though. I know you do not tell me things because you don't want to worry me.

I know you will blossom there, though things may be difficult for you now. It is always hard to be away from your homeland. The first year is always the worst, I think. We are all fine. Don't worry about anything here. And please make sure to get enough sleep.

You will see that four years will zoom by. Before you know it, we will be talking face to face.

Your loving mother

4 sad

5 gloomy

I felt melancholy[4] after reading Mother's letter. Despite her reassurances, I could tell that things were difficult back home. I pictured her worried expression, and my brothers' somber[5] faces. I was glad that I had never mentioned anything about my scholarship work in the dining hall, my need to work for pocket money, and my late nights finishing my school work. I was ashamed at not being there to help Mother through her hardships. I knew how much she had always missed my sister, her firstborn, and how she must miss me. Now, she had no daughters at home.

Through her letter, I felt her love and concern for me. But what comforted me most was her deep faith and trust. She was sure I would succeed in America, and would come back to her.

Wiping away the tears that had filled my eyes, I opened my books and began to study. *I must do well on my history test tomorrow. I must make Mother proud of me.*

About the Author

Sook Nyul Choi was born in Pyongyang, Korea, and came to the United States to go to college. She taught elementary school for twenty years and also taught creative writing to high school students. Ms. Choi's *Year of Impossible Goodbyes* is an earlier autobiographical account of ten-year-old Sookan.

Responding to the Story

▼ Think Back

How do Sookan's mother and brothers feel about Sookan's going to college in America?

What are some feelings that Sookan has as she receives and reads her mother's letter?

What kind of person is Sookan's mother? Make a list of four or five adjectives that describe what she is like.

▼ Discuss

What information did Sookan's mother include in her letter? Why was the letter important to Sookan? Why is writing letters a good way to communicate?

Is Sookan's mother correct when she says, "Just as water runs down, so does love"? How does this story illustrate that saying?

▼ Write

Write a Postcard Sookan's mother says that the family read her postcards aloud. With a partner, discuss how Sookan might answer her mother's letter. Then write a postcard from Sookan to her family.

Keep in Touch Write a postcard of your own to someone you haven't seen for a while. Before you write, think about the person and about what you want to tell him or her. Make some notes on what you've done or thoughts you've had that you would like to share.

The Telephone

Edward Field

My happiness depends on an electric appliance

And I do not mind giving it so much credit

With life in this city being what it is

Each person separated from friends

By a tangle of subways and buses

Yes my telephone is my joy

It tells me that I am in the world and wanted

It rings and I am alerted to love or gossip

I go comb my hair which begins to sparkle

Do you like getting telephone calls? Or does the sound of a ringing telephone sometimes bother you?

Without it I was like a bear in a cave

Drowsing through a shadowy winter

It rings and spring has come

I stretch and amble out into the sunshine

Hungry again as I pick up the receiver

For the human voice and the good news of friends

About the Author

Edward Field was born in 1924 in Brooklyn, New York. He achieved success with a poetry collection, *Stand Up, Friend, With Me.* He is also interested in the culture of native peoples and was the editor of *Eskimo Songs and Stories*, a collection of poems and stories.

Responding to the Poem

▼ Think Back

Where does the speaker live? Why has this location made the speaker dependent on the telephone?

How does the ringing telephone make the speaker feel?

The speaker says that without a telephone, "I was like a bear in a cave/Drowsing through a shadowy winter." Explain the comparison. In what way was the speaker like a bear in the winter?

▼ Discuss

The speaker of the poem relies on the telephone to communicate with the outside world. What is your favorite way to communicate with friends? Explain why.

Compare communicating by telephone with having a face-to-face conversation. How are the two conversations alike? How are they different?

▼ Write

Imagery The poet uses vivid images to create mental pictures that show how the speaker reacts to the ringing telephone. Make a list of the words and phrases in the poem that create these images.

It's for You What do you think about using the telephone? Would you rather call people or write to them? How much time do you spend on the phone? Write a short essay about you and your telephone.

The Letter "A"

Christy Brown

Christy Brown was born on June 5, 1932, with cerebral palsy. At that time, people did not understand birth defects or disabilities. Most children like Christy were put in special homes to be taken care of. But Christy's mother wanted him to stay with his own family. She believed that although his body was disabled, his mind was not.

Christy was unable to talk. His upper body was paralyzed, so he couldn't use his hands to sign or write. When he was five, something happened that changed Christy's life.

Christy Brown could see and hear what was going on around him, but he couldn't talk or write. How do you think he felt when he finally was able to communicate?

I was now five, and still I showed no real sign of intelligence. I showed no apparent interest in things except with my toes—more especially those of my left foot. Although my natural habits were clean, I could not aid myself, but in this respect my father took care of me. I used to lie on my back all the time in the kitchen or, on bright warm days, out in the garden, a little bundle of crooked muscles and twisted nerves, surrounded by a family that loved me and hoped for me and that made me part of their own warmth and humanity. I was lonely, imprisoned in a world of my own, unable to communicate with others, cut off, separated from them as though a glass wall stood between my existence and theirs, thrusting me beyond the sphere of their lives and activities. I longed to run about and play with the rest, but I was unable to break loose from my bondage.[1]

Then, suddenly, it happened! In a moment everything was changed, my future life molded into a definite shape, my mother's faith in me rewarded and her secret fear changed into open triumph.

It happened so quickly, so simply after all the years of waiting and uncertainty, that I can see and feel the whole scene as if it had happened last week. It was the afternoon of a cold, gray December day. The streets outside glistened with snow, the white sparkling flakes stuck and melted on the windowpanes and hung on the boughs of the trees like molten silver. The wind howled dismally, whipping up little whirling columns of snow that rose and fell at every fresh gust. And over all, the dull, murky sky stretched like a dark canopy,[2] a vast infinity[3] of grayness.

Inside, all the family were gathered round the big kitchen fire that lit up the little room with a warm glow and made giant shadows dance on the walls and ceiling.

In a corner Mona and Paddy were sitting, huddled together, a few torn school primers before them. They were writing down little sums on to an old chipped slate, using a bright piece of yellow chalk. I was

[1] physical restraint

[2] cover
[3] endless space

close to them, propped up by a few pillows against the wall, watching.

It was the chalk that attracted me so much. It was a long, slender stick of vivid yellow. I had never seen anything like it before, and it showed up so well against the black surface of the slate that I was fascinated by it as much as if it had been a stick of gold.

Suddenly, I wanted desperately to do what my sister was doing. Then—without thinking or knowing exactly what I was doing, I reached out and took the stick of chalk out of my sister's hand—with my left foot.

I do not know why I used my left foot to do this. It is a puzzle to many people as well as to myself, for, although I had displayed a curious interest in my toes at an early age, I had never attempted before this to use either of my feet in any way. They could have been as useless to me as were my hands. That day, however, my left foot, apparently by its own volition,[4] reached out and very impolitely took the chalk out of my sister's hand.

[4] will to do something

I held it tightly between my toes, and, acting on an impulse, made a wild sort of scribble with it on the slate. Next moment I stopped, a bit dazed, surprised, looking down at the stick of yellow chalk stuck between my toes, not knowing what to do with it next, hardly knowing how it got there. Then I looked up and became aware that everyone had stopped talking and was staring at me silently. Nobody stirred. Mona, her black curls framing her chubby little face, stared at me with great big eyes and open mouth. Across the open hearth, his face lit by flames, sat my father, leaning forward, hands outspread on his knees, his shoulders tense. I felt the sweat break out on my forehead.

My mother came in from the pantry with a steaming pot in her hand. She stopped midway between the table and the fire, feeling the tension flowing through the room. She followed their stare and saw me in the corner. Her eyes looked from my face down to my foot, with the chalk gripped between my toes. She put down the pot.

Then she crossed over to me and knelt down beside me, as she had done so many times before.

"I'll show you what to do with it, Chris," she said, very slowly and in a queer, choked way, her face flushed as if with some inner excitement.

Taking another piece of chalk from Mona, she hesitated, then very deliberately drew, on the floor in front of me, *the single letter "A"*.

"Copy that," she said, looking steadily at me. "Copy it, Christy."

I couldn't.

I looked about me, looked around at the faces that were turned towards me, tense, excited faces that were at that moment frozen, immobile, eager, waiting for a miracle in their midst.

⁵ complete; total

The stillness was profound.⁵ The room was full of flame and shadow that danced before my eyes and lulled

⁶ strained; tense

my taut⁶ nerves into a sort of waking sleep. I could hear the sound of the water tap dripping in the pantry, the loud ticking of the clock on the mantelshelf, and the soft hiss and crackle of the logs on the open hearth.

I tried again. I put out my foot and made a wild jerking stab with the chalk, which produced a very crooked line and nothing more. Mother held the slate steady for me.

———————

```
"Copy that," she said,
  looking steadily at me.
    "Copy it, Christy."
        I couldn't.
```

———————

"Try again, Chris," she whispered in my ear. "Again."

I did. I stiffened my body and put my left foot out again, for the third time. I drew one side of the letter. I drew half the other side. Then the stick of chalk broke and I was left with a stump. I wanted to fling it away and give up. Then I felt my mother's hand on my shoulder. I tried once more. Out went my foot. I shook, I sweated and strained every muscle. My hands were so tightly clenched that my fingernails bit into the flesh. I set my teeth so hard that I nearly pierced my lower lip. Everything in the room swam till the faces around me were mere patches of white. But—I drew it—*the letter "A"*. There it was on the floor before me. Shaky, with awkward, wobbly sides and a very uneven center line.

But it *was* the letter "A". I looked up. I saw my mother's face for a moment, tears on her cheeks. Then my father stooped and hoisted me on to his shoulder.

I had done it! It had started—the thing that was to give my mind its chance of expressing itself. True, I couldn't speak with my lips. But now I would speak through something more lasting than spoken words—written words.

That one letter, scrawled on the floor with a broken bit of yellow chalk gripped between my toes, was my road to a new world, my key to mental freedom. It was to provide a source of relaxation to the tense, taut thing that was I, which panted for expression behind a twisted mouth.

About the Author

Christy Brown (1932-1981) was an Irish poet and author. Brown was born in Dublin, the tenth of twenty-two children. With the help of his family and doctors, he overcame his disability. When he was 18 he learned to talk. Christy turned out to have a highly imaginative mind and was able to express himself in poetry and novels. "The Letter 'A'" is an excerpt from his autobiography, *My Left Foot,* which was made into a movie starring Daniel Day Lewis.

Responding to the Autobiography

▼ Think Back

What was Christy's life like before he learned to write?

What nonverbal clues does Christy Brown's family give as he tries to write for the first time?

What does Christy feel and hear as he tries to write?

▼ Discuss

What does Christy Brown mean when he says that the letter *A* was his "key to mental freedom"?

How did Christy's family treat him? How do you think their attitudes helped him learn to communicate?

▼ Write

Sensory Language Sensory language appeals to one of the five senses—sight, hearing, smell, taste, or touch. Christy Brown's descriptions of the weather and the rooms in the Brown house are filled with vivid sensory language. Work with a group of classmates to find sensory descriptions in "The Letter 'A.'" Make lists under headings for the five senses.

Describe a Place Write a page or two describing a place. Use sensory language to help the reader see, hear, smell, taste, or touch what the place is like.

Twenty Questions

Erma Bombeck

Parents and teens often have a hard time talking with each other. This mother asks questions and hopes for answers!

Next to having my teeth cleaned without a sedative, my second favorite thing is playing Twenty Questions with my teenage son at one in the morning. It is like carrying on a conversation with a computer with a dead battery.

"Is that you, Roger?" I shout from the bedroom.

"Who do you think it is?"

"What time is it?"

"What time do you think it is?" he answers.

"Did I hear the clock strike one?"

"What clock?"

"The one in the hallway. Did you have a good time at the dance?"

"Dance?"

"You know, the one you went to. Was it jammed?"

"Who told you it was jammed?"

"No one told me," I shouted. "I'm asking. I suppose you got a pizza afterward?"

"How did you know?"

"I can smell it. A pizza sinks into your pores. You can smell it until the next shower."

"You want me to take a shower at this time of night?"

"No. I said when you eat a pizza it sinks into your pores, which you can smell until the next shower."

"What's that got to do with the dance being crowded?"

"Nothing," I sighed. "Do you want anything to eat?"

"On top of the pizza?"

"Then you did have pizza. Did you see Marcia?"

"Marcia who?"

"YOUR SISTER, MARCIA."

"Was I supposed to?"

"You mean both of you were at the same dance and you didn't talk to one another?"

"What's to talk about?" he asked.

"Is that the clock dinging again?"

"What clock?"

"The one in the hallway. Did you let the dog out?"

"Why?"

"I thought I heard something scratching."

"Want me to check it?" he queried.

"Would you see if it's Marcia?"

"What would she be doing scratching on the door?"

"Is it the dog then?" I asked.

"Is that something to call your daughter?"

"What are you talking about?" I asked.

"What are you talking about?" He responded.

"Did you hang up your clothes?"

"Can't I do it tomorrow?"

"Do you know how much I spend in cleaning bills because you don't hang up your clothes?"

"How much?"

"Don't be cute. How late is it?"

"How late is what?"

"The hour. I think you are trying to keep the time from me, aren't you?"

"Why would I want to do that?"

"Because it is late," I said.

"Who said it was late?" he asked.

"Didn't I just hear the clock chime?"

"What clock?"

"Roger! Exactly what time is it?"

He was asleep. He had tricked me again. I had had my Twenty Questions and he had responded with his Twenty Questions. I was wide awake.

My husband rolled over restlessly. "Is that you babbling?" he asked.

"Who do you think it is?" I snapped.

"What time is it?" he yawned.

"What time do you think it is?" I retorted.

"I don't really care," he said and drifted off.

I shook him by the throat. "Wake up! You've got eighteen more questions to ask or you're out of the game!"

About the Author

Erma Bombeck (1927–1996), described herself as a housewife, garbage hustler, and pretty face. Her sense of humor was applauded by the thousands of people who read her nationally syndicated column, "At Wit's End."

Responding to the Essay

▼ Think Back

What does Roger's mother hope to find out?

How does Roger respond to his mother's questioning?

Why is the mother frustrated at the end of the essay?

▼ Discuss

Roger probably thinks he had a conversation with his mother. What do you think? What kind of relationship do you think Roger and his mother have? Why?

Is there a "communication gap" between adults and teenagers? What makes you think as you do? Why do you think such a gap might exist?

▼ Write

Write an Essay Can you recall a discussion you had with a parent or another adult? Was the discussion satisfying for one or both of you? Why or why not? Write a short essay describing what the discussion was about. Be sure to use a little humor.

Write a Conversation One of the reasons why "Twenty Questions" is so enjoyable is because Erma Bombeck treats the topic with a great deal of humor. Work with a partner to write your own version of a conversation. Decide what role each of you will play—adult, child, friend, teacher, brother, or so on. Write your conversation, then practice reading your lines aloud.

Happy Birthday

Toni Cade Bambara

Have you ever wanted to shout to the world that it's your birthday? Ollie has something like that in mind.

[1] person in charge of taking care of the building

O llie spent the whole morning waiting. First she tried shaking Granddaddy Larkins, who just wouldn't wake up. She thought he was just playing, but he was out. His teeth weren't even in the glass, and there was a bottle on the bedstand. He'd be asleep for days. Then she waited on the cellar steps for Chalky, the building superintendent,[1] to get through hauling garbage and come talk. But he was too busy. And then Ollie sat on the stairs waiting for Wilma. But it was Saturday and Wilma'd be holed up somewhere stuffing herself with potato chips and crunching down on jaw breakers, too greedy to cool it and eat 'em slow. Wilma'd come by tomorrow, though, and lie her behind off. "I went to Bear Mountain yesterday on a big boat with my brother Chestnut and his wife," she'd say, "and that's why I didn't come by for you cause we left so early in the morning that my mother even had to get me up when it was still dark out and we had a great time and I shot bows and arrows when we got there, and do you like my new dress?" Wilma always had some jive tale and always in one breath.

Ollie tried to figure out why she was even friends with Wilma. Wilma was going to grow up to be a lady and marry a doctor and live in New York, Wilma's mother said. But Ollie, poor orphan, was going to grow up and marry a drinking man if she didn't get killed first, Wilma's mother said. Ollie never told Granddaddy Larkins what Wilma's mother was all the time saying. She just hated her in private.

Ollie spent the early afternoon sitting on the rail in front of The Chicken Shack Restaurant, watching the cooks sling the wire baskets of chicken in and out of the frying fat. They were too sweaty and tired to tell her to move from in front. "Ruining the business," the owner used to fuss. Later she stood between the laundry and shoe store, watching some men pitch pennies against the building. She waited for a while, squeezing a rubber ball in her hand. If I can just get the wall for a minute, she thought, maybe somebody'll come along and we'll have us a good game of handball. But the men went right on pitching while other ones were waiting their turn. They'd be there for hours, so Ollie left.

She knocked on Mrs. Robinson's door to see if she wanted her dog walked. It was cool in the hallway at least. No one was home, not even the loud-mouth dog that usually slammed itself against the door like he was big and bad instead of being just a sorry little mutt. Then Ollie took the stairs two at a time, swinging up past the fourth floor to the roof. There was rice all over.

Ronnie must have already fed his pigeons. The door to the roof was unlocked, and that meant that the big boys were on the roof. She planted her behind against the door and pushed. She kicked at a cluster of rice. Some grains bounced onto the soft tar of the roof and sank. When Ollie moved onto the roof, the blinding sun made her squint. And there they were, the big boys, jammed between the skylight and the chimney like dummies in a window, just doing nothing and looking half-asleep.

Peter Proper, as always, was dressed to the teeth. "I naturally stays clean," he was always saying. Today he said nothing, just sitting. Marbles, a kid from the projects, had an open book on his knees. James was there, too, staring at a fingernail. And Ferman, the nut from crosstown, and Frenchie, the athlete. A flurry of cinders floated down from the chimney and settled into their hair like gray snow.

"Why don't you just sit in the incinerator?[2] You can get even dirtier that way," Ollie yelled. No one moved or said anything. She expected Frenchie to at least say, "Here comes Miss Freshmouth," or for Peter to send her to the store for eighteen cents' worth of American cheese. It was always eighteen cents' worth, and he always handed her a quarter and a nickel. Big Time. "Don't none of you want nothing from the store today?" She squinted with her hands on her hips, waiting for the store dummies to start acting like Marbles, Peter, James, and so forth.

[2] large container for burning trash

Ferman straightened out a leg against the skylight. "Ollie, when are you going to learn how to play with dolls?"

"Ya want anything from the store, Ferman Fruitcake? I'm too big for dolls." Ollie hitched up her jeans.

Ferman started to say something, but his audience was nearly asleep. Frenchie's head was nodding. James was staring into space. The pages of the open book on Marbles' knees were turning backward, three at a time, by themselves. Peter Proper was sitting very straight, back against the chimney with his eyes closed to the sun.

Ollie turned, looking over the edge of the roof. There was no one down in the park today. There was hardly anyone on the block. She propped a sticky foot against the roof railing and scraped off the tar. Everything below was gray as if the chimney had snowed on the whole block.

Chalky, the superintendent, was rolling a mattress onto a cart. Maybe he'd play cards with her. Just last Friday he had, but sometimes he wouldn't even remember her and would run and hide thinking she was King Kong come down just to hit him in the head or something. Ollie looked past the swings to the track. Empty. Frenchie should be out there trotting, she thought, looking back at him. He was dipping his head. Sometimes she'd trot beside Frenchie, taking big jumps to keep up. He'd smile at her but never teased her about them silly little jumps. He'd tell her for the hundredth time how he was going to enter the Olympics and walk off with a cup full of money.

"Go away, little girl!" Ferman had just yelled at her as if he had forgotten her name or didn't know her any more. He's as crazy as Chalky, thought Ollie, slamming the big roof door behind her and running down the stairs to the street. They must be brothers.

It was now four o'clock by the bank clock. Ollie remembered the bar-b-que place that had burned down. But she'd already rummaged through the ruins and found nothing. No use messing up her sneakers any further. She turned around to look the block over. Empty. Everyone was either at camp or at work or was sleeping like the boys on the roof or dead or just plain gone off. She perched on top of the fire hydrant with one foot, balancing with her arms. She could almost see into the high windows of Mount Zion A.M.E. Church. "This time I'm going to fly off and kill myself," she yelled, flapping her arms. A lady with bundles turned the corner and gave Ollie a look, crossed against the traffic, looking over her shoulder and shaking her head at what the kids of today had come to. Reverend Hall came out of the church basement, mopping his head with a big handkerchief.

"You go play somewhere else," he said, frowning into the sun.

"Where?" Ollie asked.

"Well, go to the park and play."

"With who?" she demanded. "I've got nobody to play with."

Reverend Hall just stood there trying to control his temper. He was always chasing the kids. That's why he's got no choir, Granddaddy Larkins was always saying. He always chases kids and dogs and pigeons and drunks.

"Little girl, you can't act up here in front of the church. Have you no—"

"How come you always calling me little girl, but you sure know my name when I'm walking with my grandfather?" Ollie said.

"Tell'm all about his sanctified[3] self," said Miss Hazel, laughing out her window. But when the Reverend looked up to scowl, she ducked back in. He marched back into the church, shooing the pigeons off the steps.

[3] holier-than-thou; acting as if better than anyone

"Wish me happy birthday," Ollie whispered to the pigeons. They hurried off toward the curb. "Better wish me happy birthday," she yelled, "or somebody around here is gonna get wasted."

Miss Hazel leaned out the window again. "What's with you, Ollie? You sick or something?"

"You should never have a birthday in the summertime," Ollie yelled, "cause nobody's around to wish you happy birthday or give you a party."

"Well, don't cry, sugar. When you get as old as me, you'll be glad to forget all about—"

"I'm not crying." Ollie stamped her foot, but the tears kept coming and before she could stop herself she was howling, right there in the middle of the street and not even caring who saw her. And she howled so loudly that even Miss Hazel's great-grandmother had to come to the window to see who was dying and with so much noise and on such a lovely day.

"What's the matter with the Larkins child?" asked the old woman.

"Beats me." Miss Hazel shook her head and watched Ollie for a minute. "I don't understand kids sometimes," she sighed, and closed the window so she could hear the television good.

About the Author

Toni Cade Bambara was born in 1939 in New York City. She grew up in Harlem, Bedford-Stuyvesant, and Queens, as well as Jersey City, New Jersey. Bambara credits her mother for much of her success, and the musicians of the 1940s and 1950s with the rhythm of her writing. She advises other writers to experiment with writing materials—rice paper, bamboo drawing sticks, brown wrapping paper, different kinds of pens—until they find those that suit them.

Responding to the Story

▼ Think Back

Does Ollie have a large family? Who does she live with? What is he doing on her birthday?

What time of year does the story take place? How does this help explain the way people act?

List some people Ollie tries to communicate with. When people do talk to her what kinds of things do they say?

▼ Discuss

What causes Ollie to wonder why she is friends with Wilma? Why doesn't she like Wilma's mother?

Miss Hazel says that she "doesn't understand kids sometimes." Do you understand Ollie? Why is she making so much noise crying on such a lovely day?

Do you get the feeling that people dislike Ollie? Why do you think everyone ignores her? Why doesn't she tell people it's her birthday?

▼ Write

Continue the Story Suppose that Ollie sees Wilma the next day and tells her about her birthday. What do you think Ollie would say? Write a page giving Ollie's version of what she did. Make sure it sounds like Ollie.

Surprise! What if all those people were just pretending and they knew about Ollie's birthday all along? Write a new, happy ending for the story.

Theme Links

Communication

In this unit, you've explored some of the ways people communicate, or try to communicate, with each other. You have also thought about how important it is to share your ideas and feelings with others.

▼ Group Discussion

With a partner or in a small group, talk about the selections in this unit and how they relate to the theme and to your own lives. Use questions like the following to guide the discussion.

- What are some ways that people you read about in this unit communicated with one another? Why did some of them have problems communicating?
- What are some other ways of communicating?
- After reading these selections, are you more likely to express your ideas and feelings to others or encourage your friends to express theirs? Why or why not?

▼ Meet the Characters

With a partner or in a small group, think about the selections in the unit. Is there a character or person whom you think didn't get heard or who has a lot more to say? What would that character say if he or she had the opportunity? Write a scene that presents additional thoughts and feelings of a character. Then role-play the scene for the whole class.

Which two characters would you like to introduce? Suppose you have introduced them. Write a conversation between the two characters or have one character write a letter to the other.

▼ History of Communication

With your class, create a museum exhibit showing the ways you and your friends communicate. First create a list, then work on gathering the items or photographs that represent them. Your exhibit can include any of the following:

- videos
- computer
- fax machine
- telephone
- fliers
- posters/signs
- pager/beeper
- mail/letter
- newsletter/newspaper

For each display, write an accompanying caption card that describes the significance and impact—positive or negative—that the device has on how you communicate.

▼ The Theme and You

Is there something that excites, troubles, puzzles, or amuses you that you are hesitant to discuss with others? Perhaps writing down your thoughts and feelings will motivate you to discuss the subject with your family or friends. Write an essay in which you communicate your feelings and ideas about a topic. Share your essay with a classmate and then discuss the topic.

Decisions

You make many decisions every day. Some are small decisions, such as what to wear or where to go after school. Others are important decisions that make a difference in your life. These decisions can shape your character and help you find out what's most important to you.

Making decisions can be scary because only you are responsible for what happens as a result of what you decide. Think about a decision you made that changed something in your life. Would your decision be the same if you had it to do over again? Why or why not?

The selections in this unit are about people who either have to make important decisions or are learning to live with decisions they have already made. As you read, think about why each person makes the decision he or she does. Then think about what you take into consideration when faced with an important decision.

Early Autumn

Langston Hughes

After years of not seeing each other, Bill and Mary meet again. What goes through their minds?

[1] suddenly and without much thought

[2] without thinking

When Bill was very young, they had been in love. Many nights they had spent walking, talking together. Then something not very important had come between them, and they didn't speak. Impulsively,[1] she had married a man she thought she loved. Bill went away, bitter about women.

Yesterday, walking across Washington Square, she saw him for the first time in years.

"Bill Walker," she said.

He stopped. At first he did not recognize her, to him she looked so old.

"Mary! Where did you come from?"

Unconsciously,[2] she lifted her face as though wanting a kiss, but he held out his hand. She took it.

"I live in New York now," she said.

"Oh"—smiling politely. Then a little frown came quickly between his eyes.

"Always wondered what happened to you, Bill."

"I'm a lawyer. Nice firm, way downtown."

"Married yet?"

"Sure. Two kids."

"Oh," she said.

A great many people went past them through the park. People they didn't know. It was late afternoon. Nearly sunset. Cold.

"And your husband?" he asked her.

"We have three children. I work in the bursar's[3] office at Columbia."

[3] treasurer's

"You're looking very . . ." (he wanted to say *old*) ". . . well," he said.

She understood. Under the trees in Washington Square, she found herself desperately reaching back into the past. She had been older than he then in Ohio. Now she was not young at all. Bill was still young.

"We live on Central Park West," she said. "Come and see us sometime."

"Sure," he replied. "You and your husband must have dinner with my family some night. Any night. Lucille and I'd love to have you."

The leaves fell slowly from the trees in the Square. Fell without wind. Autumn dusk. She felt a little sick.

"We'd love it," she answered.

"You ought to see my kids." He grinned.

Suddenly the lights came on up the whole length of Fifth Avenue, chains of misty brilliance in the blue air.

"There's my bus," she said.

He held out his hand, "Good-by."

"When . . ." she wanted to say, but the bus was ready to pull off. The lights on the avenue blurred, twinkled, blurred. And she was afraid to open her mouth as she entered the bus. Afraid it would be impossible to utter a word.

Suddenly she shrieked very loudly, "Good-by!" But the bus door had closed.

The bus started. People came between them outside, people crossing the street, people they didn't know. Space and people. She lost sight of Bill. Then she remembered she had forgotten to give him her address—or to ask him for his—or tell him that her youngest boy was named Bill, too.

About the Author

Langston Hughes (1902–1967) was not only a leading African-American poet and writer of fiction, but also a song lyricist, newspaper columnist, and playwright. He also edited six anthologies of African-American literature.

Responding to the Story

▼ Think Back

Why is it surprising that both Bill and Mary are living in New York City?

How does Bill feel about Mary? Is he still in love with her? How do you know?

The last sentence of the story states that Mary named her youngest son Bill. What does this tell you about her feelings for Bill?

▼ Discuss

Langston Hughes could have had the story take place at any time of year and day in any kind of weather. But he chose to have Bill and Mary meet on a cold fall day as the sun is setting. Why?

What decision did Mary make years ago? How does she feel about that decision now? How can you tell? How did Mary's decision affect Bill?

▼ Write

Dear Diary Imagine that you are Mary. Write a diary entry about what it was like to see Bill again. Or write a few sentences that Bill might write in his diary about the meeting.

Write a Conversation Think of someone from your past that you would like to see again. What would the two of you do and say if you ran into each other? Write a one or two page story that includes a conversation.

Joe

Sherry Garland

Loi is the daughter of an American soldier and a Vietnamese mother. The thing Loi values most is a picture of her father. She hopes to go to the United States someday and find him. Now Loi is seventeen. Her family wants her to marry a man she doesn't love. Loi runs away to Ho Chi Minh City with her boyfriend Khai. When they are separated, Loi must continue on her own.

Have you ever been angry at someone, yet also felt sorry for that person? That is a problem the girl in this story faces.

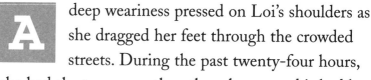 deep weariness pressed on Loi's shoulders as she dragged her feet through the crowded streets. During the past twenty-four hours, she had slept no more than three hours, and it had been a restless sleep at that. Now, faced with the uncertainty of her future, she found it more and more difficult to lift her feet.

When Loi finally reached the building with the tall steeple, she felt as if she had come to a roadside rest stop during a long journey. She sank into the cool grass under a tall eucalyptus tree in a small park across the street from the massive stone building with the stained-glass windows. Not far from her feet, clumps of bright yellow chrysanthemums filled the air with their musty fragrance and a cluster of red bottlebrush trees attracted hordes of honeybees.

As the dappled light flickered across her eyes and a light breeze lapped away her perspiration, Loi began to think about Khai. He had said he would catch the next bus to Saigon. She wasn't sure when that would be, but surely no more than one day. Da Lat was a popular tourist town to which many Saigonese traveled for vacations or honeymoons. But once he arrived in Saigon, how would they find each other? Should she wait for him at the bus station, or should she go ahead and register at the Foreign Office and wait for him there? Khai had heard the American tell her that was the place to go; maybe he would try to find her there as soon as he arrived. Loi began to relive the last time she had seen Khai and the look of pain in his eyes as he reached for her fingers. She whimpered under her breath, then fell into the deep sleep of exhaustion.

Loi wasn't sure how long she had been sleeping when something scampered across her chest. Her dream told her it was the rats that often tried to steal her mother's rice bag from a pole in the little hut. Loi smiled in her sleep, thinking she was once again on the cot next to her cousins. But then the scamper became a rough pain on the back of her neck, as if someone were pulling her hair. With a little cry, she sat up and rubbed her stinging neck.

For a moment Loi didn't understand where she was. She heard fleeing footsteps and saw a boy with orange-colored hair running across the park carrying something in his hand. Loi stood but something felt wrong. She glanced down at her chest.

"My sack!" she cried in terror.

With a shot of speed, Loi took off after the boy. He had a good lead on her, but her legs were long and used to running down the country lanes after rabbits and dogs. She leapt over the short wrought-iron fence of the park, cutting in and out of the flower beds. Her heart pounded in her ears and her lungs filled to capacity with hot air. All the while she chased the culprit, she chastised[1] herself for being so stupid as to leave her cloth pouch in plain sight while she slept. She knew better than that. She also knew better than to leave the money and cigarettes in the sack; they should have been safely tucked inside her secret pocket. But worst of all, the photo of her American father wrapped in the piece of blue silk was in that pouch, carelessly shoved back in after the last time she looked at it. She would never, never forgive herself for losing that. Without the photo, how could she prove to the authorities that she was half American?

With a fear greater than she had ever known, even greater than the time she had confronted a cobra in the rice paddy, Loi found a second wind and caught up with the boy as he tripped over a man working on a broken bicycle in the middle of the sidewalk. With a scream, Loi stretched her long arms toward the boy's neck and seized his shirt collar.

[1] blamed; criticized

"Help! Murder! Murder!" he shouted in a squeaky voice that was in the throes[2] of changing from boy to man.

[2] a condition of struggle

A few people laughed, but no one seemed to believe him. The bike repairman cursed and threatened to crack the boy's head open with his wrench.

```
"You're crazy, girl! This
   is my bag. My poor old
widowed mother sewed it up
for me a year ago. I carry
  it with me all the time."
```

"Give me back my pouch, or you will be crying more than murder," Loi said between clenched teeth as she tried to get a better hold on his twisting, skinny body.

"You're crazy, girl! This is my bag. My poor old widowed mother sewed it up for me a year ago. I carry it with me all the time."

"Ha! You little liar. Tell me what's inside it."

"Uh—" He held it close to his face. "Rice!" His eyes twinkled as he grinned triumphantly.

"Anyone could smell that. What else?"

"Uh—tobacco."

"Another lucky guess. That only proves you have a good nose, even though, I must admit, it is the ugliest nose I have ever seen. It's a nose any water buffalo would be proud of, however."

The boy's grin turned into a scowl and his bare feet kicked Loi's shins ferociously.

"Hey, little rabbit-thief. That's what you are . . . like a rabbit trying to steal my cabbages and kicking when you're caught. But kicks won't help you today." Loi grabbed for the sack, but the boy stuffed it inside his shabby shirt and twisted free. He bolted down the street.

With a silent curse, Loi struck out after him again, only to lose him when he vanished around a corner. For a few minutes she searched in vain for his orange hair. Her heart was starting to ache with anguish,[3] when she heard his familiar screams.

[3] sorrow; anxiety

"Help! Murder! Murder!"

With a smile, Loi plowed her way through the crowd in the direction of the noise. She stumbled to a halt in front of a small man with close-set, mean eyes who was wearing a tan uniform with red epaulettes.[4] His air of authority made the warning about the police from the old man on the bus suddenly ring in her ears, and she stepped back. But her eyes remained fixed on the sack swinging in the officer's left hand. In his other hand, the boy-thief swung at the air and cursed with words Loi had never imagined. When the boy saw her, he stopped struggling and waved her over.

[4] fancy shoulder pads on the outside of a garment

"Sister, sister, come quickly. This policeman thinks I stole this bag. Tell him the truth."

"Is this your brother's sack, *con-lai*?"[5]

[5] *Vietnamese*: half-breed; a child of parents from different races

A shiver ran through Loi's body at the insult, but she nodded.

"Ha! I think you both stole it. Can you prove it's yours?" The angry scowl on the policeman's face prevented Loi from speaking.

"Yes, she can prove it. Go ahead, sister, tell him what's inside the bag. Remember, rice, tobacco . . ."

"A little carving. And a photograph of my American father."

The uniformed man opened the bag, unwrapped the blue cloth, and took out the photograph. A wicked smile curled on his lips as he looked at it, then he spat into the street. He shoved the picture back into the bag and rummaged until he found the opened pack of cigarettes. He casually shook out a handful, then tossed the bag at Loi's feet.

"Stay away from here, you fatherless thieves. Go back to your mother or I'll throw you in jail and send you off to reeducation camp." He stomped his foot, as if chasing away a mongrel cur, and the boy ran.

Loi picked up the sack and ran toward the steeple—the only place she felt safe. When she finally stopped, she took out the pack of cigarettes and counted them—only ten left. With a sigh, she dropped to the soft green grass and leaned against the eucalyptus tree again. She removed the photo and studied the tall man with the smiling face and curly hair, standing beside her short mother.

"Why did you come here?" she whispered. "My mother was so happy before you came. If you had left her alone, I wouldn't be here now, sitting under a tree with no home."

"Is that really your American father?"

Loi looked up at the orange-haired boy standing very quietly behind her.

"What do you care who this is?" she muttered and rewrapped it carefully. This time she tucked it inside the pocket sewn to the inside of her waistband.

"My father was American, too," he said with a shrug, then squatted down beside her.

Loi scrutinized[6] his shamelessly ugly face. The broad nose looked more like it belonged to a *moi*[7] tribesman. And the spots on it did not look natural, like her freckles. They were smeared and uneven, as if painted on. His hair, orange and frizzy, was the most unhuman hair she had ever seen. She couldn't imagine how it had ended up in such a condition, but she knew he could not have been born with that hair, for the roots were very black.

"You don't look part American," she finally replied.

"Well, I am," he insisted and stuck his chin out. "Where do you think I got my brown hair and freckled nose?"

"I think you got the freckles from a paintbrush. And only heaven can say how your hair got to be such an awful color of streaked orange."

"Brown! My hair is brown! And curly, like yours."

"All right, all right. Say what you wish. But that still doesn't give you the right to steal my pouch. All I own is inside here."

The boy cocked his head a moment, studying her from under half-closed eyes. Then he grinned and thrust

[6] studied; examined closely

[7] *Vietnamese:* a mountain tribesman; (insulting term, meaning "savage")

out his hand. Loi stared at it in amazement. What did he expect her to do with the grime-covered thing?

"Gimme five," he said in English.

"What did you say?"

"It's what they say in America. It means, 'Shake my hand.'"

"Why would I want to touch your filthy hand?"

"Don't act like a stupid country girl. That's what Americans do when they meet somebody. They shake hands. Come on, *gimme five*."

Loi gingerly reached out and touched the boy's fingers, then quickly withdrew her hand in repulsion.[8]

[8] distaste; a feeling of disgust

"What's your name, farm girl?"

"Pham Thi Loi."

"Miss Loi! What an old-fashioned name. Sounds just like something a farm girl would have."

Loi jumped to her feet.

"I was not born on a farm. My mother lived in a big city when I was born. Da Nang. My name is just as good as yours. What is your name anyway, city thief-boy?"

"Joe. Just call me Joe."

"What kind of crazy name is that? It sounds Chinese."

"Don't you know anything about America, girl? Joe is the number-one name for boys. Everybody calls everybody Joe."

"And how do you know so much about America?"

"I told you, my father was American."

"Ha! My mother told me all the Americans left when I was a baby. You're only about twelve years old, the same age as my cousin Dinh. You couldn't have an American father."

"That's what many people say. But my story is unusual."

Loi shook her head. "*You* are unusual, Mr. Joe. Can you tell me the directions to the Foreign Office?"

"You're going to register to go to America?" His dark eyes lit up, and he leapt to his feet.

"Yes. I was on my way there when a certain little thief-boy stole my food sack and got me all turned around in this too-big city. Now I don't know which way to go."

"Don't worry," Joe said as he put his hand on her back and began to steer her across the park. "I know everything there is to know about the Foreign Office and going to America. I'm going, too, you know."

Loi raised one eyebrow.

"You've already registered?" she asked.

"Well . . . not exactly," he said as they began slowly walking down a tree-lined avenue, dodging bicycles. "You see, no one in the Office believes that I'm really half American. It's because I'm so young, you know. But my story is unusual. I keep telling them my father was an *M-I-A*—"

"What is an *M-I-A*?"

"A soldier that got lost and never made it back to America when everybody else left. You see, my father lived in the jungle many years. My lovely mother found him bitten by a snake and sucked the poison from his leg. Then she took care of him in her little hut at the foot of the mountain."

"What kind of snake?"

"A . . . a python, I think it was called."

"Oh, Joe. Pythons aren't poisonous. They wrap themselves around their prey and crush the bones. My uncle caught one once by biting its tail. That makes it let go and . . ."

"Let me finish my story! Who cares what kind of snake it was! Then she took care of him, and he fell in love with her. After I was born and a few years old, one day he said to her, 'I can't live in this jungle anymore. I miss America. I miss *baseball*—'"

"*Baseball?* What is—"

"Shhh! 'I miss *hotdog* and *John Wayne* movie and *Madonna* tapes. Sorry, beautiful lady of the jungle and handsome little baby boy, but I have to get back to my wife and three kids.'"

"What?"

"So my mother, being like an angel, said, 'I love you so much, I will sacrifice my own happiness and help you get back to America.' And she sewed up a skirt and shirt like a Black Thai tribesman's and painted his face brown and walked with him all the way to the border of China."

"China! But isn't China almost two thousand miles away?"

"Maybe it was Cambodia. I was just a child. But my lovely mother was so sad and missed him so much that she left me on the doorstep of that big Catholic church over there, then threw herself into the river. But before she died, she said, 'Joe, you go to America and find your father. Tell him I loved him so much I could not live without him.'"

Joe reached up and pretended to wipe away a tear, but Loi saw no sign of water in his eyes.

"Hmmmph! No wonder the Foreign Office doesn't believe that fairy tale. I bet you don't even have a photo or letter or anything proving your father was American, do you?"

"My sweet angel mother put the only photo she had inside her blouse when she dove into the raging river. It washed away on big bubbles."

"I thought you were on the church doorstep." Loi shook her head, then burst into laughter.

"Why are you laughing? Everything is true, believe me. My mother really did throw herself into the Saigon River."

"I don't doubt that. But more likely it was because she saw your ugly face when you were born."

Joe crossed his arms and turned his back. "I thought you were my friend," he said in a quivery voice. Soon he made loud sobs.

Loi felt a twinge of guilt run through her heart. At least he hadn't insulted her for being a *con-lai*. He was the first person she had ever met who *wanted* to be part American.

"Oh, all right. I'm sorry, Joe. It's a wonderful story. And your mother was an angel."

Joe whirled around with a grin on his face and dry eyes.

"Say, why don't you be my sister?" He reached up and put his hand on her shoulder. "We can go to America together. You can tell the Foreign Office that the man in your photo is my father, too."

"I already have a cousin your age. Why should I want a brother, too? Especially one as ugly as you."

Joe halted in his tracks and crossed his arms again. Loi stopped and turned around.

"Well? What's wrong now?"

"I'm not going to show you where the Foreign Office is."

"All right, all right, all right. I'm sorry I called you ugly. You're as handsome as the Jade Emperor's son," she said, but secretly she thought about when the Jade Emperor's son came to earth disguised as an ugly frog.

Joe kept his feet planted and stubbornly shook his orange hair.

"I don't care what you call me. I want to be your brother. If you don't claim me for a brother, I won't show you where the Foreign Office is."

"I can ask somebody else. Lots of people know where it is."

"Yes, but do they know exactly what to do? Do they know the names of the men in the Office and how to act and every little secret trick? Do you think that you have to fill out only one little form? Country girl, there are so many forms it would make your head swim. Some to send to the Americans in Bangkok, some for here, some for Hanoi. Without me you're gonna have to wait in line for days."

"Days!" Loi looked at his set chin and clenched lips, then shrugged. "All right, come on, little orange-haired brother."

Joe flashed his white grin, then ran up to Loi and thrust out his dirty hand.

"*Gimme five,* big sister!"

About the Author

Sherry Garland writes for both children and young adults. Her interest in Vietnam came about as she helped Vietnamese immigrants in her community. She wrote a nonfiction book on the subject, *Vietnam: Rebuilding a Nation,* and was inspired by a picture of an Amerasian child to write *Song of the Buffalo Boy* from which "Joe" is taken.

Responding to the Story

▼ Think Back

How does Loi meet Joe? What kind of person is Joe?

Why did Loi leave home? Where is she going and why?

Is Joe really part American? What details give you clues about Joe's past?

▼ Discuss

The policeman who helps Loi get her bag back insults her because she is part American. Why do you think he has contempt for Loi, even though she has no control over who her parents are?

Why do you think Loi decides to help Joe? Do you agree with her decision? Why or why not?

▼ Write

Plot the Story A story is built around a character with a goal and some conflict, or problem, that keeps the character from reaching that goal. The plot of a story includes all the events that happen. In a small group, complete a story map for "Joe." Identify Loi's goal, the story events, and the problems or conflicts that keep her from reaching her goal.

Write a Letter How do you think Loi's mother feels about her running away? Write a letter from Loi to her mother explaining why she left her village and what has happened to her in Saigon.

The Courtship

George Ella Lyon

Jim is a widower who sets out to find a wife. Why doesn't he give her much time to make up her mind?

When Sickly Jim Wilson's first wife died
he tried to carry on
keep house and farm his scrabbly land
and it like to broke him.
All them kids were too old to stay put
and too young to carry water. There was no one
to cook, wash, or sew, no one but Sickly Jim
and him the same body who must milk the cow
and plant the scanty hay. Soon he saw
he had to have another wife.

[1] possible candidates for a position

He considered the prospects[1] on the creek,
listed them according to his favor:
Widow Jones, Miss Creech, the oldest Phillips girl,
and even Mossie Maggern. The thought of Mossie
made his belly cold, but next morning he set out.

Widow Jones was stringing beans on her hillside
porch. He rode right up to the rail.

"Morning Miz Jones. How are you now?"
"Working steady," was her answer,
"and how about yourself?" "Not faring well,
not faring well at all. If I'm to farm
and raise my kids, I've got to have a helpmeet.
That's why I'm here. It looks to me
like you might be the one. What do you say?"

She studied him, walked to the edge of the porch.
"I didn't think wives were got
the way a man gets pigs or harness.
I thought it usually took a little time
and a feller got off his horse."
"You know, Miz Jones, I mean no offense[2]   [2] insult
but time's a thing I've run short of.
I've got babies crying at home
and so I speak out plain."
"Well give me the day. You come back
around suppertime for my answer."
"No ma'am. I need a wife before that."
He looked at the paper in his hand.
"You're the first on my list, but if you
can't oblige, I'll be off to try Miss Creech."

He settled his hat, turned his horse,
and was almost out of the yard
when she called to him, "I've given it thought.
It's clear I'm the wife you need.
Hold till Sunday and I'll marry you."
And that's just what she did.

Responding to the Poem

▼ Think Back

What makes Sickly Jim Wilson decide he needs to look for a new wife?

How does Jim go about getting a wife?

Why do you think Widow Jones agrees to marry Jim Wilson?

▼ Discuss

Given the circumstances, do you think Jim Wilson's attitude and haste to get a wife are justified? Why or why not?

Why is "The Courtship" a good title for this poem?

▼ Write

Spread the News Write a short news article for the local paper reporting on the wedding of Sickly Jim Wilson and Widow Jones. Remember to include information that answers the questions Who? What? Where? When? and Why?

Continue the Poem What do you think happens after Jim and Widow Jones are married? Write at least two more stanzas for the poem telling about the wedding or the couple's new life.

One Throw

W. C. Heinz

I checked into a hotel called the Olympia, which is right on the main street and the only hotel in the town. After lunch I was hanging around the lobby, and I got to talking to the guy at the desk. I asked him if this wasn't the town where that kid named Maneri played ball.

"That's right," the guy said. "He's a pretty good ballplayer."

"He should be," I said. "I read that he was the new Phil Rizzuto." [1]

"That's what they said," the guy said.

"What's the matter with him?" I said, "I mean if he's such a good ballplayer what's he doing in this league?"

"I don't know," the guy said. "I guess the Yankees know what they're doing."

"What kind of a kid is he?"

"He's a nice kid," the guy said. "He plays good ball, but I feel sorry for him. He thought he'd be playing

Have you ever wished for a lucky break that would change your life? This story is about a minor-league baseball player who's waiting for his lucky break—a chance to play in the majors.

[1] a star shortstop for the New York Yankees during the 1940s and 1950s

One Throw **135**

for the Yankees soon, and here he is in this town. You can see it's got him down."

"He lives here in this hotel?"

"That's right," the guy said. "Most of the older ballplayers stay in rooming houses,[2] but Pete and a couple other kids live here."

[2] houses with rooms that renters can live in

He was leaning on the desk, talking to me and looking across the hotel lobby. He nodded his head. "This is a funny thing," he said. "Here he comes now."

The kid had come through the door from the street. He had on a light gray sport shirt and a pair of gray flannel slacks.

I could see why, when he showed up with the Yankees in spring training, he made them all think of Rizzuto. He isn't any bigger than Rizzuto, and he looks just like him.

"Hello, Nick," he said to the guy at the desk.

"Hello, Pete," the guy at the desk said. "How goes it today?"

"All right," the kid said, but you could see he was exaggerating.

"I'm sorry, Pete," the guy at the desk said, "but no mail today."

"That's all right, Nick," the kid said. "I'm used to it."

"Excuse me," I said, "but you're Pete Maneri?"

"That's right," the kid said, turning and looking at me.

"Excuse me," the guy at the desk said, introducing us. "Pete, this is Mr. Franklin."

"Harry Franklin," I said.

"I'm glad to know you," the kid said, shaking my hand.

"I recognize you from your pictures," I said.

"Pete's a good ballplayer," the guy at the desk said.

"Not very," the kid said.

"Don't take his word for it, Mr. Franklin," the guy said.

"I'm a great ball fan," I said to the kid. "Do you people play tonight?"

"We play two games," the kid said.

"The first game's at six o'clock," the guy at the desk said. "They play pretty good ball."

"I'll be there," I said. "I used to play a little ball myself."

"You did?" the kid said.

"With Columbus," I said. "That's twenty years ago."

"Is that right?" the kid said. . . .

That's the way I got to talking with the kid. They had one of those pine-paneled taprooms[3] in the basement of the hotel, and we went down there. I had a couple and the kid had a Coke, and I told him a few stories and he turned out to be a real good listener.

"But what do you do now, Mr. Franklin?" he said after a while.

"I sell hardware," I said. "I can think of some things I'd like better, but I was going to ask you how you like playing in this league."

"Well," the kid said, "I suppose it's all right. I guess I've got no kick[4] coming."

[3] bars

[4] complaint

"Oh, I don't know," I said. "I understand you're too good for this league. What are they trying to do to you?"

"I don't know," the kid said. "I can't understand it."

"What's the trouble?"

"Well," the kid said, "I don't get along very well here. I mean there's nothing wrong with my playing. I'm hitting .365 right now. I lead the league in stolen bases. There's nobody can field with me, but who cares?"

"Who manages this ball club?"

"Al Dall," the kid said. "You remember, he played in the outfield for the Yankees for about four years."

"I remember."

"Maybe he is all right," the kid said, "but I don't get along with him. He's on my neck all the time."

"Well," I said, "that's the way they are in the minors sometimes. You have to remember the guy is looking out for himself and his ball club first. He's not worried about you."

"I know that," the kid said. "If I get the big hit or make the play he never says anything. The other night I tried to take second on a loose ball and I got caught in the run-down. He bawls me out in front of everybody. There's nothing I can do."

"Oh, I don't know," I said. "This is probably a guy who knows he's got a good thing in you, and he's looking to keep you around. You people lead the league, and that makes him look good. He doesn't want to lose you to Kansas City or the Yankees."

"That's what I mean," the kid said. "When the Yankees sent me down here they said, 'Don't worry. We'll keep an eye on you.' So Dall never sends a good report on me. Nobody ever comes down to look me over. What chance is there for a guy like Eddie Brown or somebody like that coming down to see me in this town?"

"You have to remember that Eddie Brown's the big shot," I said, "the great Yankee scout."

"Sure," the kid said. "I never even saw him, and I'll never see him in this place. I have an idea that if they ever ask Dall about me he keeps knocking me down."

"Why don't you go after Dall?" I said. "I had trouble like that once myself, but I figured out a way to get attention."

"You did?" the kid said.

"I threw a couple of balls over the first baseman's head," I said. "I threw a couple of games away, and that really got the manager sore. I was lousing up his ball club and his record. So what does he do? He blows the whistle on me, and what happens? That gets the brass[5] curious, and they send down to see what's wrong."

[5] top management

"Is that so?" the kid said. "What happened?"

"Two weeks later," I said, "I was up with Columbus."

"Is that right?" the kid said.

"Sure," I said, egging him on. "What have you got to lose?"

"Nothing," the kid said. "I haven't got anything to lose."

"I'd try it," I said.

"I might try it," the kid said. "I might try it tonight if the spot comes up."

I could see from the way he said it that he was madder than he'd said. Maybe you think this is mean to steam a kid up like this, but I do some strange things.

"Take over," I said. "Don't let this guy ruin your career."

"I'll try it," the kid said. "Are you coming out to the park tonight?"

"I wouldn't miss it," I said. "This will be better than making out route sheets and sales orders."

It's not much of a ball park in this town—old wooden bleachers and an old wooden fence and about four hundred people in the stands. The first game wasn't much either, with the home club winning something like 8 to 1.

The kid didn't have any hard chances, but I could see he was a ballplayer, with a double and a couple of walks and a lot of speed.

The second game was different, though. The other club got a couple of runs and then the home club picked up three runs in one, and they were in the top of the ninth with a 3–2 lead and two outs when the pitching began to fall apart and they loaded the bases.

I was trying to wish the ball down to the kid, just to see what he'd do with it, when the batter drives one on one big bounce to the kid's right.

The kid was off for it when the ball started. He made a backhand stab and grabbed it. He was deep now, and he turned in the air and fired. If it goes over the first baseman's head, it's two runs in and a panic—but it's the prettiest throw you'd want to see. It's right on a line, and the runner is out by a step, and it's the ball game.

I walked back to the hotel, thinking about the kid. I sat around the lobby until I saw him come in, and then I walked toward the elevator like I was going to my room, but so I'd meet him. And I could see he didn't want to talk.

"How about a Coke?" I said.

"No," he said. "Thanks, but I'm going to bed."

"Look," I said. "Forget it. You did the right thing. Have a Coke."

We were sitting in the taproom again. The kid wasn't saying anything.

"Why didn't you throw that ball away?" I said.

"I don't know," the kid said. "I had it in my mind before he hit it, but I couldn't."

"Why?"

"I don't know why."

"I know why," I said.

The kid didn't say anything. He just sat looking down.

"Do you know why you couldn't throw that ball away?" I said.

"No," the kid said.

"You couldn't throw that ball away," I said, "because you're going to be a major-league ballplayer someday."

The kid just looked at me. He had that same sore[6] expression.

[6] angry

"Do you know why you're going to be a major-league ballplayer?" I said.

The kid was just looking down again, shaking his head. I never got more of a kick out of anything in my life.

"You're going to be a major-league ballplayer," I said, "because you couldn't throw that ball away, and because I'm not a hardware salesman and my name's not Harry Franklin."

"What do you mean?" the kid said.

"I mean," I explained to him, "that I tried to needle you into throwing that ball away because I'm Eddie Brown."

About the Author

W. C. Heinz was born in 1915 in Mount Vernon, New York. His newspaper career included working as a copy boy, a reporter, war correspondent, and sports columnist. He has said that he feels lucky that he grew up during "The Golden Era of Sports" and liked being a sportswriter because he got to travel with the teams and get to know them. Heinz has won many awards for his articles, novels, and short stories. He is the author of _The Professional_, considered by some to be the finest novel ever written about boxing.

Responding to the Story

▼ Think Back

Pete seems eager to know if he received any mail. What letter is he hoping to receive?

Who does Eddie Brown pretend to be? Why does he pretend to be someone else?

Eddie tells Pete about a way to get management's attention. What does Eddie tell Pete to do?

▼ Discuss

Eddie's advice to Pete can be seen as a kind of test. What is Eddie testing? Does Pete pass Eddie's test? Why or why not?

Was it wrong of Eddie to test Pete in this way? Or is it OK since, in the end, Eddie helps Pete? Explain why you think what Eddie did is right—or wrong.

▼ Write

Write a Diary Entry Imagine you are Pete. Write a diary entry explaining why you didn't throw the game and how you felt when you learned who Harry really was.

Write About an Incident Have you ever been in a situation where your integrity and honesty were tested? How did you handle it? Write a page or two describing the incident. Try to use foreshadowing to add interest to your story.

Your World

Georgia Douglas Johnson

Your world is as big as you make it.
I know, for I used to abide[1]
In the narrowest nest in a corner,
My wings pressing close to my side.

But I sighted the distant horizon
Where the skyline encircled the sea
And I throbbed with a burning desire
To travel this immensity.[2]

I battered the cordons[3] around me
And cradled my wings on the breeze
Then soared to the uttermost reaches
With rapture, with power, with ease!

We can learn by understanding other people's decisions. What did the speaker of this poem do to change her life?

[1] stay; remain

[2] vastness

[3] blockades

Responding to the Poem

▼ Think Back

To what animal does the speaker of the poem compare herself?

What causes the speaker to leave the "narrowest nest in the corner"?

How has the speaker changed at the end of the poem?

▼ Discuss

How does the rest of the poem develop the opening statement, "Your world is as big as you make it"?

What decision does the speaker make? What advice is the poet giving?

▼ Write

Find the Beat The *rhythm* of a poem is the pattern of stressed and unstressed syllables that repeat to give the poem its beat. The *rhyme scheme* is the pattern of rhyming words. Read the poem aloud while a partner writes the syllables that you stress. Then have your partner read aloud while you write the words that rhyme.

Write in Rhythm Think about a fear you have overcome or a time that you "spread your wings" and tried something new. Write a poem about the experience. Use some rhyming words and create a rhythm that gives your poem its own "beat."

Theme Links

Decisions

In this unit, you have read about some people who are making decisions and others who are living with the results of decisions they made earlier. You've seen how decisions affect people's lives and thought about the big decisions in your life.

▼ Group Discussion

With a partner or in a small group, talk about how the selections in this unit relate to the theme and to your lives. Use questions like the following to guide the discussion.

• What decision must each character make? How do their decisions affect themselves and others?

• Have you ever had to make a decision like one of these characters made? What was it? How did you decide?

• What advice would you give to a friend who must make an important decision?

▼ Different Endings

How would the stories in the unit be different if the characters had made other decisions? With a small group, pick a story to role-play a different ending. Your role-play should

• explain why the character made his or her decision

• show what happened to the main character and others

• tell what the main character and others learned.

▼ Local (Close-to-Home) Decisions

Some decisions affect more than one person or one family. They affect a whole school or community. How are those decisions made? What is the right thing to do? Think about an important issue in your school or community. Work with a group of classmates to make a recommendation. Follow these steps.

1. Research the issue to find information that explains the various viewpoints.
2. Compare your research and opinions with your group. Discuss the results.
3. Compile your research findings in an Issue Report.
4. Prepare and present a proposal to the class, stating your position and recommended decision.

▼ The Theme and You

What was the most important decision you've ever made? Think about a time in your life when you had to make a tough choice. What made the decision so difficult? Did you make the right decision? What factors did you have to consider?

Write a journal entry in which you review your decision-making process. Try to remember and record your thoughts and feelings at the time. Describe how the decision turned out and how it affected your life.

Acknowledgments

Acknowledgment is gratefully made to the following publishers, authors, and agents for permission to reprint these works. Every effort has been made to determine copyright owners. In the case of any omissions, the Publisher will be pleased to make suitable acknowledgments in future editions.

"Yes, It Was My Grandmother" from *A Breeze Swept Through* by Luci Tapahonso, West End Press, 1987. Reprinted by permission of the author.

"The Scholarship Jacket" by Marta Salinas from *Nosotras: Latina Literature Today*, edited by Maria del Carmen Boza, Beverly Silva, and Carmen Valle (1986). Reprinted by permission of Bilingual Press/Editorial Bilingüe, Arizona State University, Tempe, AZ.

"That Something Special: Dancing with the Repertory Dance Company of Harlem" by Leslie Rivera is reprinted with permission from the publisher of *Hispanic, Female and Young* (Arte Público Press—University of Houston, 1994).

"The Contest" reprinted with permission from *Singing to the World: Marian Anderson* by Janet Stevenson, © 1963 Encyclopaedia Britannica Press, Inc.

Beautiful Junk: A Story of the Watts Towers by Jon Madian. Originally published by Little Brown & Company, 1968. Revised, 1992. Reprinted with permission of the author.

"Oranges" from *New and Selected Poems* by Gary Soto © 1995, published by Chronicle Books, San Francisco.

"Andrew" from *The Mystic Adventures of Roxie Stoner* by Berry Morgan. Copyright © 1966, 1967, 1968, 1969, 1971, 1973, 1974 by Berry Morgan. Reprinted by permission of Houghton Mifflin Company. All rights reserved.

"Thank You, M'am" from *Something in Common* by Langston Hughes. Copyright © 1963 by Langston Hughes. Copyright renewed © 1991 by Arnold Rampersad and Ramona Bass. Reprinted by permission of Hill and Wang, a division of Farrar, Straus & Giroux, Inc.

Coming Home: A Dog's True Story by Ted Harriott (Victor Gollancz/Hamish Hamilton, 1985). Copyright © Ted Harriott, 1985. Reproduced by permission of Frederick Warne & Co.

"Birdfoot's Grampa" by Joseph Bruchac. Reprinted from *I Tell You Now: Autobiographical Essays by Native American Writers*, edited by Brian Swann and Arnold Krupat, by permission of the University of Nebraska Press. Copyright © 1987 by the University of Nebraska Press.

148